PRAISE FOR *GLORY DAYS*

Max Lucado has done it again! In his new book, *Glory Days*, Max is encouraging a generation of Christians to live out of their inheritance, to fight from victory, and to take God at his word. Max reminds us of all that we have in Christ and the necessity of faith and obedience in the face of trials and difficult circumstances.

> Greg Laurie, senior pastor, Harvest Christian Fellowship; founder, Harvest Crusades

At some point, many of us have wondered if this is as good as the Christian life gets. Maybe we've experienced loss or feel far away from God. In *Glory Days*, Max Lucado explains that we have an amazing Savior who is waiting for us to come to him to find freedom and victory—he wants to take us to our Promised Land. Through the story of Joshua, Max explains how we can put the past behind us and walk into the glorious life God has for us.

I believe God's anointing is on Max to write and communicate the truths of God for this generation. This book not only communicates God's heart, it is life changing, heaven altering, kingdom building, and personally edifying. This book, like all his books, will change your life.

> Robert Morris, founding senior pastor, Gateway Church; and bestselling author, *The Blessed Life*, *From Dream to Destiny*, and *Truly Free*

In classic Lucado style, *Glory Days* unpacks what it means to know that God fights for you—and how that knowledge will change every part of your life. This is a message the Church needs and a reminder every believer can use.

> Mark Batterson, *New York Times* bestselling author, *The Circle Maker*; and lead pastor, National Community Church

Thank you, brother Max, for laying out the pathway to knowing a fulfilling and glorious life in Christ in such a clear and readable way. To the reader, do with this book as Elijah did with the water when rebuilding the altar of God's glory on Mt. Carmel. Read it, read it, and read it again. Then step back from all human effort and pray. Watch the Glory of God fill your life again.

   | Carter Conlon, senior pastor, Times Square Church

GLORY DAYS

ALSO BY MAX LUCADO

INSPIRATIONAL

3:16

A Gentle Thunder

A Love Worth Giving

And the Angels Were Silent

Before Amen

Come Thirsty

Cure for the Common Life

Facing Your Giants

Fearless

God Came Near

God's Story, Your Story

Grace

Great Day Every Day

He Chose the Nails

He Still Moves Stones

In the Eye of the Storm

In the Grip of Grace

It's Not About Me

Just Like Jesus

Max on Life

Next Door Savior

No Wonder They Call Him the Savior

On the Anvil

Outlive Your Life

Six Hours One Friday

The Applause of Heaven

The Great House of God

Traveling Light

When Christ Comes

When God Whispers Your Name

You'll Get Through This

FICTION

Christmas Stories

The Christmas Candle

Miracle at the Higher Grounds Cafe

BIBLES (GENERAL EDITOR)

Grace for the Moment Daily Bible

The Lucado Life Lessons Study Bible

Children's Daily Devotional Bible

CHILDREN'S BOOKS

A Max Lucado Children's Treasury

Do You Know I Love You, God?

God Forgives Me, and I Forgive You

God Listens When I Pray

Grace for the Moment: 365 Devotions for Kids

Hermie, a Common Caterpillar

Itsy Bitsy Christmas

Just in Case You Ever Wonder

Lucado Treasury of Bedtime Prayers

One Hand, Two Hands

Thank You, God, for Blessing Me

Thank You, God, for Loving Me

The Boy and the Ocean

The Crippled Lamb

The Oak Inside the Acorn

The Tallest of Smalls

You Are Mine

You Are Special

YOUNG ADULT BOOKS

3:16

It's Not About Me

Make Every Day Count

Wild Grace

You Were Made to Make a Difference

GIFT BOOKS

Fear Not Promise Book

For the Tough Times

God Thinks You're Wonderful

Grace for the Moment

Grace for the Moment Morning and Evening

Grace Happens Here

His Name Is Jesus

Let the Journey Begin

Live Loved

Mocha with Max

Safe in the Shepherd's Arms

This Is Love

You Changed My Life

GLORY DAYS

LIVING YOUR PROMISED LAND LIFE NOW

MAX LUCADO

THOMAS NELSON
Since 1798

Published in Nashville, Tennessee, by Thomas Nelson. Thomas Nelson is a registered trademark of HarperCollins Christian Publishing, Inc.

Thomas Nelson titles may be purchased in bulk for educational, business, fundraising, or sales promotional use. For information, please e-mail SpecialMarkets@ThomasNelson.com.

Unless otherwise noted, Scripture quotations are taken from the New King James Version®. © 1982 by Thomas Nelson. Used by permission. All rights reserved.

Other Scripture references are from the following sources: THE AMPLIFIED BIBLE: OLD TESTAMENT (AMP). © 1962, 1964 by Zondervan (used by permission). THE AMPLIFIED BIBLE: NEW TESTAMENT (AMP). © 1958 by the Lockman Foundation (used by permission). THE CONTEMPORARY ENGLISH VERSION (CEV). © 1995 by the American Bible Society. Used by permission. English Standard Version (ESV). © 2001 by Crossway Bibles, a division of Good News Publishers. God's Word (GOD'S WORD) is a copyrighted work of God's Word to the Nations Bible Society. Quotations are used by permission. © 1995 by God's Word to the Nations Bible Society. All rights reserved. King James Version (KJV). *The Message* (MSG) by Eugene H. Peterson. © 1993, 1994, 1995, 1996, 2000, 2001, 2002. Used by permission of NavPress Publishing Group. All rights reserved. New American Standard Bible® (NASB). © The Lockman Foundation 1960, 1962, 1963, 1968, 1971, 1972, 1973, 1975, 1977, 1995. Used by permission. New Century Version® (NCV). © 2005 by Thomas Nelson. Used by permission. All rights reserved. Holy Bible, New International Version®, NIV® (NIV). Copyright © 1973, 1978, 1984, 2011 by Biblica, Inc.™ Used by permission of Zondervan. All rights reserved worldwide. www.zondervan.com. *Holy Bible*, New Living Translation (NLT). © 1996, 2004, 2007, 2013. Used by permission of Tyndale House Publishers, Inc., Wheaton, Illinois 60189. All rights reserved. New Revised Standard Version of the Bible (NRSV). © 1989 by the Division of Christian Education of the National Council of the Churches of Christ in the U.S.A. All rights reserved. J. B. Phillips: THE NEW TESTAMENT IN MODERN ENGLISH (PHILLIPS). © J. B. Phillips 1962. Used by permission of Macmillan Publishing Co., Inc. *The Living Bible* (TLB). © 1971. Used by permission of Tyndale House Publishers, Inc., Wheaton, Illinois 60189. All rights reserved.

ISBN: 978-0-7180-3896-0 (IE)
ISBN: 978-0-7180-7714-3 (SE)

Library of Congress Control Number: 2015935254

ISBN: 978-0-8499-4849-7

Printed in the United States of America

15 16 17 18 19 RRD 6 5 4 3 2

For LeeEric Fesko and Elizabeth Johnson
with immense gratitude for your selfless
service and steady leadership

These days are Glory Days.
My past is past,
my future is bright,
God's promises are true and
his Word is sure.
With God as my helper,
I will be all he wants me to be,
do all he wants me to do,
and receive all he wants me to receive.
These days are Glory Days.

CONTENTS

ACKNOWLEDGMENTS

This book exists because these people, day in and day out, show up, make good decisions, offer valuable edits, and know when to give me a kick or a hug. You'll find their pictures hanging on the walls of the publishing Hall of Fame.

Editors: Liz Heaney, Karen Hill, Carol Bartley, and David Drury

Management and lifelong friends: Steve and Cheryl Green

TNI publishing team: Mark Schoenwald, David Moberg, Laura Minchew, and dozens of other fine folks who manage, market, and administer

Marketing geniuses: Greg and Susan Ligon, Jana Muntsinger, and Pamela McClure

Radio ministry partnership: Peggy Campbell, Evelyn Gibson, and the Ambassador Advertising Agency team

Oak Hills Church family and coworkers, especially Randy Frazee, Mark Tidwell, Janie Padilla, Margaret Mechinus, and Dave Treat

And then there is my family: Brett, Jenna, Andrea, Jeff, Sara, and Andy. You put the joy in my heart.

And my wonderful wife, Denalyn. What Joshua did for the Hebrews, you do for me every day. You lead me out of the wilderness. Love you forever.

I

———

GLORY DAYS

For seven years they were virtually untouchable.

Seven nations conquered. At least thirty-one kings defeated. Approximately ten thousand square miles of choice property claimed.

Seven years of unbridled success.

They were outnumbered but not outpowered. Underequipped but not overwhelmed. They were the unlikely but unquestionable conquerors of some of the most barbaric armies in history. Had the campaign been a prizefight, the referee would have called it in the first round.

The Hebrew people were unstoppable.[1]

They hadn't always been. The Bible doesn't gloss over the checkered history of God's chosen people. Abraham had too many wives. Jacob told too many lies. Esau sold his birthright. Joseph's brothers sold Joseph. Four centuries of Egyptian bondage were followed by forty years of wilderness wandering. Then later, seventy years of Babylonian detention.

The Hebrew people built two temples only to lose them. They were given the ark of the covenant only to lose it. Babylonia built her cities. Greece flexed her muscles. Rome stretched her empire. And

Israel? In the schoolroom of ancient societies, she was the kid with the black eye, bullied and beat-up.

Except for those seven years. The Glory Days of Israel. On the time line of your Bible, the era glistens between the difficult days of Exodus and the dark age of the judges. Moses had just died, and the Hebrews were beginning their fifth decade as bedouin in the badlands. And sometime around 1400 BC,[2] God spoke, Joshua listened, and the Glory Days began. The Jordan River opened up. The Jericho walls fell down. The sun stood still, and the kings of Canaan were forced into early retirement. Evil was booted and hope rebooted. By the end of the campaign, the homeless wanderers became hope-filled homesteaders. A nation of shepherds began to quarry a future out of the Canaanite hills. They built farms, villages, and vineyards. The accomplishments were so complete that the historian wrote:

> So the LORD gave to Israel all the land of which He had sworn to give to their fathers, and they took possession of it and dwelt in it. The LORD gave them rest all around, according to all that He had sworn to their fathers. And not a man of all their enemies stood against them; the LORD delivered all their enemies into their hand. Not a word failed of any good thing which the LORD had spoken to the house of Israel. All came to pass. (Josh. 21:43–45)

What sweeping statements! "The LORD gave . . . all the land." "The LORD gave them rest." "Not a man of all their enemies stood against them." "All came to pass." Winter chill gave way to springtime thaw, and a new season was born.

Perhaps you need a new season as well. You don't need to cross the Jordan River, but you need to get through the week. You aren't facing Jericho, but you are facing rejection or heartache. Canaanites don't stalk you, but disease, discouragement, danger? Rampant. You wonder if you have what it takes to face tomorrow.

You can relate to the deflated little fellow I saw in an airport terminal. He and his family were on summer vacation. At least that's what I Sherlocked from the way they were dressed. Flip-flops, baseball caps, and straw hats. They were beach-bound for a week of sand and sun.

Everything about the dad's expression said, "Hurry up! We have to run if we are going to make the connection!" The concourse was his football field and the departure gate his end zone. He was determined to score a touchdown.

Can the little fellow keep up? I wondered. Mom could. She matched her husband stride for stride. The big brothers could. They hitched their backpacks higher and leaned forward into the draft of their parents.

But the little guy? He was five years old, six at most. His face was resolved, but his legs were so short. It didn't help matters that he was dragging a pint-size Mickey Mouse carry-on bag. Nor did it help that the entire civilized world was jammed into the airport. He tried to match his parents' pace, but he just couldn't.

So he stopped. Right in the middle of the mayhem, he gave up. He plopped his bag on the floor, sat on top of it, and shouted in the direction of his disappearing family, "I can't keep up!"

Can you relate?

Sometimes the challenge is just too much. You want to keep up. You try. It's not that you don't. You just run out of fight. Life has a way of taking the life out of us.

The book of Joshua is in the Bible for such seasons. It dares us to believe our best days are ahead of us. God has a Promised Land for us to take.

The Promised Land was the third stop on the Hebrews' iconic

itinerary. Their pilgrimage began in Egypt, continued through the wilderness, and concluded in Canaan. Each land represents a different condition of life. Geography is theology. In Egypt the Hebrews were enslaved to Pharaoh. In the wilderness they were free from Pharaoh but still enslaved to fear. They refused to enter the Promised Land and languished in the desert. Only in Canaan did they discover victory. Egypt, the wilderness, and Canaan. Slaves to Pharaoh, slaves to fear, and, finally, people of the promise.

We too have traveled this itinerary. Egypt represents our days before salvation. We were in bondage to sin. We wore the leg irons of guilt and death. But then came our Deliverer, Jesus Christ. By his grace and in his power, we crossed the Red Sea. He liberated us from the old life and offered a brand-new life in Canaan.

Our Promised Land isn't a physical territory; it is a spiritual reality. It's not real estate but a real state of the heart and mind.

A Promised Land life in which "we are more than conquerors through [Christ] who loved us" (Rom. 8:37).

A life in which "we do not lose heart" (2 Cor. 4:16).

A life in which "[Christ's] love has the first and last word in everything we do" (2 Cor. 5:14 MSG).

A life in which we are "exceedingly joyful in all our tribulation" (2 Cor. 7:4).

A life in which we are "anxious for nothing" (Phil. 4:6), in which we are "praying always" (Eph. 6:18), in which we "do all in the name of the Lord Jesus, giving thanks to God the Father through Him" (Col. 3:17).

Canaan is a life defined by grace, refined by challenge, and aligned with a heavenly call. In God's plan, in God's *land*, we win more often than we lose, forgive as quickly as we are offended, and give as abundantly as we receive. We serve out of our giftedness and delight in our assignments. We may stumble, but we do not collapse.

We may struggle, but we defy despair. We boast only in Christ, trust only in God, lean wholly on his power. We enjoy abundant fruit and increasing faith.

Canaan symbolizes the victory we can have today. In spite of what the hymn suggests—"To Canaan's land I'm on my way, where the soul of man never dies"[3]—Canaan is not a metaphor for heaven. The idea is beautiful, but the symbolism doesn't work. Heaven will have no enemies; Canaan had at least seven enemy nations. Heaven will have no battles. Joshua and his men fought at least thirty-one (Josh. 12:9–24). Heaven will be free of stumbles and struggle. Joshua's men weren't. They stumbled and struggled, but their victories far outnumbered their defeats.

Canaan, then, does not represent the life to come. Canaan represents the life we can have now!

God invites us to enter Canaan. There is only one condition. We must turn our backs on the wilderness.

Just as Canaan represents the victorious Christian life, the wilderness represents the *defeated* Christian life. In the desert the Hebrew people were liberated from Egyptian bondage, but you wouldn't have known it by listening to them. Just three days into their freedom "the people complained against Moses, saying, 'What shall we drink?'" (Ex. 15:24).

A few more days passed, and "the children of Israel complained against Moses and Aaron in the wilderness . . . 'Oh, that we had died by the hand of the LORD in the land of Egypt . . . For you have brought us out into this wilderness to kill this whole assembly with hunger'" (16:2–3).

"The people contended with Moses" (17:2), and "the people complained against Moses" (v. 3). They inhaled anxiety like oxygen. They bellyached to the point that Moses prayed, "What shall I do with this people? They are almost ready to stone me!" (v. 4).

How did the Hebrews descend to this point? It wasn't for the lack of miracles. They saw God's power in high definition. They watched locusts gobble crops, boils devour skin, flies buzz through Pharaoh's court. God turned the chest-thumping Egyptians into shark bait right before the Hebrews' eyes. But when God called them to cross over into Canaan, the twelve spies returned, and all but two said the mission was impossible. The giants were too big for them. "We were like grasshoppers," they said (Num. 13:33). *We were tiny, tiny bugs. They will squash us.*

So God gave them time to think it over. He put the entire nation in time-out for nearly forty years. They walked in circles. They ate the same food every day. Life was an endless routine of the same rocks, lizards, and snakes. Victories were scarce. Progress was slow. They were saved but not strong. Redeemed but not released. Saved from Pharaoh but stuck in the desert. Redeemed but locked in a routine. Monotonous. Dull. Ho-hum, humdrum. Four decades of tedium.

Sounds miserable.

It might sound familiar.

I sat across the lunch table today from a man in midlife misery. He described his life with words like *stuck, rut,* and *stalled out.* He's a Christian. He can tell you the day he escaped Egypt. But he can't tell you the last time he defeated a temptation or experienced an answered prayer. Twenty years into his faith he fights the same battles he was fighting the day he came to Christ. He's out of Egypt, but Egypt's not out of him.

He didn't say the words, but I could sense the sentiment: "I thought the Christian life would be better than this." He feels disengaged and discouraged. It's as if the door to spiritual growth has a lock and everyone has the key but him. He doesn't know whom to blame. Himself? The church? God? He doesn't know what to do.

Change congregations? Change Bible translations? Slow down and reflect? Get busy and work?

My friend is not alone in the wilderness. The REVEAL Research Project went on a search for Joshuas. Beginning in 2007 they surveyed the members of more than a thousand churches. They wanted to determine the percentage of churchgoers who are actually propelled by their faith to love God and love others with their whole hearts. How many Christians would describe their days as Glory Days?

The answer? Eleven percent.[4]

Eleven percent! Nearly nine out of ten believers, in other words, languish in the wilderness. Saved? Yes. Empowered? No. They waste away in the worst of ways—in the Land of In-Between. Out of Egypt but not yet in Canaan.

Eleven percent! If a high school graduated only 11 percent of its students, if a hospital healed only 11 percent of its patients, if a baseball team won only 11 percent of its games, if a home builder completed only 11 percent of his projects, wouldn't changes be made?

The church has a serious deficiency.

We also have a wonderful opportunity. About 2.2 billion people on our planet call themselves Christians. That is approximately one-third of the world's population.[5] If the survey is any indication, about 2 billion of those Christians are chugging along on a fraction of their horsepower. Such sluggishness can only lead to weak churches and halfhearted ministries. What would happen if they got a tune-up? How would the world be different if 2 billion people came out of the wilderness? How much joy would be unleashed into the atmosphere? How much wisdom would be quarried and shared? How many marriages would be saved? How many wars would be prevented? How much hunger would be eliminated? How many orphanages would be built? How many orphanages would we need? If every Christian began to live the Promised Land life, how would the world be different?

If you began to live the Promised Land life, how would you be different? Do you sense a disconnect between the promises of the Bible and the reality of your life? Jesus offers abundant joy. Yet you live with oppressive grief. The Epistles speak of grace. You shoulder such guilt. We are "more than conquerors" (Rom. 8:37) yet are commonly conquered by temptations or weaknesses.

Caught in the land between Egypt and Canaan.

Think about the Christian you want to be. What qualities do you want to have? More compassion? More conviction? More courage? What attitudes do you want to discontinue? Greed? Guilt? Endless negativity? A critical spirit?

Here is the good news. You can. With God's help you can close the gap between the person you are and the person you want to be, indeed, the person God made you to be. You can live "from glory to glory" (2 Cor. 3:18). The walls of Jericho are already condemned. The giants are already on the run. The deed to your new life in Canaan has already been signed. It just falls to you to possess the land.

Joshua and his men did this. They went from dry land to the Promised Land, from manna to feasts, from arid deserts to fertile fields. They inherited their inheritance. Their epitaph deserves a second reading.

> So the LORD gave to Israel all the land of which He had sworn to give to their fathers, and they took possession of it and dwelt in it. The LORD gave them rest all around, according to all that He had sworn to their fathers. And not a man of all their enemies stood against them; the LORD delivered all their enemies into their hand. Not a word failed of any good thing which the LORD had spoken to the house of Israel. All came to pass. (Josh. 21:43–45)

Personalize that promise. Put your name in the blanks.

The Lord gave to _____ all the life he had sworn to give. And
_____ took possession of it and dwelt in it. The Lord gave
_____ rest all around and not an enemy stood. Not a word
failed of any good thing which the Lord had spoken to _____.
All came to pass.

This is God's vision for your life. Imagine the thought. You at full throttle. You as you were intended. You as victor over the Jerichos and giants.

You and your Promised Land life.

It is yours for the taking.

Expect to be challenged. The enemy won't go down without a fight. But expect great progress. Life is different on the west side of the Jordan. Breakthroughs outnumber breakdowns. God's promises outweigh personal problems. Victory becomes, dare we imagine, a way of life. Isn't it time for you to change your mailing address from the wilderness to the Promised Land? Your Glory Days await you.

Ready to march?

2

INHERIT YOUR INHERITANCE

Joshua 1:1–6

The time has come to attack the disease. It has raged, untouched, too long. Infected, unhindered, too many. Misery bobs in its wake. Abandoned dreams, ravaged marriages, truncated hopes. Hasn't the malady contaminated enough lives?

Time to declare war on the pestilence that goes by the name "I can't."

It attacks our self-control: "I can't resist the bottle." Careers: "I can't keep a job." Marriages: "I can't forgive." Our faith: "I can't believe God cares for me."

"I can't." The phrase loiters on the corner of Discouragement and Despair. Had Joshua mumbled those words, who would have blamed him? His book begins with bad news: "After the death of Moses the servant of the LORD" (Josh. 1:1).

There was no one like Moses. When the Hebrew people were enslaved, Moses confronted Pharaoh. When the Red Sea raged, Moses prayed for help. When the ex-slaves were hungry, thirsty, or confused, Moses intervened, and God provided food, water, and the Ten Commandments. Moses meant more to the Hebrews than Queen Victoria, Napoleon, and Alexander the Great meant to their people. Even George Washington shares Mount Rushmore with three other presidents. If Moses' face were carved into Mount Sinai, the Hebrews would never let another share the honor with him. To lose Moses was to lose the cause.

And they lost him. Moses died.

Oh, the dismay, the grief, the fear. And yet, with the grass yet to grow over Moses' grave, God told Joshua, "Moses . . . is dead. Now therefore, arise" (v. 2).

We would take a different tack. "Moses is dead. Now therefore, grieve . . . retreat . . . reorganize . . . find a therapist." But God said, "Now therefore, arise."

Already we are getting hints of a major theme in Joshua: God's power alters the score. Moses may be dead, but God is alive. The leader has passed, but the Leader lives on.

Even so, Joshua had reason to say "I can't." Two million reasons. According to a census in the book of Numbers, there were 601,730 men aged twenty and older, not counting the Levites, who crossed into Canaan.[1] Assuming that two-thirds of these men had a wife and three children, the number was about two million Hebrews. Joshua was not leading a Boy Scout troop through Canaan. This population was the size of the city of Houston.

Two million *inexperienced* Hebrews. They had never passed this way before. They could fight snakes, leopards, and windstorms. But breach the walls of Jericho? Resist the iron-wheeled chariots of the Canaanites? Wage war on the bloodthirsty barbarians across the river?

Perizzites, Hittites, Canaanites, Amorites . . . just odd names to us. But names that struck fear in the hearts of the Hebrew people. These tribes were a cesspool of evil. They appear on the pages of Scripture as early as the promise of God to Abram:

———

Know certainly that your descendants will be strangers in a land that is not theirs, and will serve them, and they will afflict them four hundred years . . . But . . . they shall return here, for the iniquity of the Amorites is not yet complete. (Gen. 15:13, 16)

For eight centuries the Amorites had cultivated a culture of degradation. They sacrificed babies in worship. They practiced orgies in the city and dedicated themselves to witchcraft and idolatry. One scholar called the Canaan of thirteenth century BC a "snake pit of child sacrifice and sacred prostitution, . . . [people who were] ruthlessly devoted to using the most innocent and vulnerable members of the community (babies and virgins) to manipulate God or gods for gain."[2] The Book of Jubilees, written probably in the second century BC, called the Amorites "an evil and sinful people whose wickedness surpasses that of any other, and whose life will be cut short on earth."[3]

Yet another reason Joshua could have said "I can't."

Excuse #1: "Moses is dead." Excuse #2: "My people are battlefield tenderfeet." Excuse #3: "Canaanites eat folks like us for breakfast."

But he never declared defeat. Before Joshua could assemble any fears, God gave him reason for faith. "Arise, go over this Jordan, you and all this people, to the land which I am giving to them" (Josh. 1:2).

Not "the land I *might* give them."

Not "the land you must conquer."

Not "the land of which you must prove worthy."

Not "the land you must earn, confiscate, or purchase."

But "the land which I am giving to them."

The transaction had already happened. The land had already been transferred. The conquest was a fait accompli. Joshua wasn't sent to take the land but to receive the land God had taken. Victory was certain because the victory was God's.

Hmmm.

My dad said something similar to me when I was sixteen years old. Our family was seated at the dinner table when the oddest thing happened. Somewhere between the passing of the peas and the beans, a set of car keys appeared next to my plate.

The ensuing dialogue went something like this:

MAX: What are these keys?
DAD: Keys to a Plymouth Belvedere that is parked out front in the driveway.
MAX: Whose car is it?
DAD: Yours.
MAX: Are you serious?
DAD: As a heart attack.
MAX: *Gulp*

I had asked my dad for a car every day of my life. In my sonogram picture I am holding up a sign that says "Car, please?" Most babies cry, "Mama!" I cried, "Mustang!"

My father's stock reply to my pleading was "You'll have a car once you earn it, qualify for it, save for it, take out a loan for it, receive a government grant for it, pay for it." I had been led to believe that a car acquisition was my job.

But then came that wonderful, glorious night when Dad handed me the keys. The company for which he worked had a car auction, and he, in a moment of weakness, bought one for me. Consequently, he gave me not payment vouchers or requirements but keys. "Take the car I am giving you."

I had a new car because he declared it.

The Hebrews had a new land because their Father did the same. About the time Joshua lifted his jaw off the ground, God explained the dimensions of the gift:

> Every place that the sole of your foot will tread upon I have given you, as I said to Moses. From the wilderness and this Lebanon as far as the great river, the River Euphrates, all the land of the Hittites, and to the Great Sea toward the going down of the sun, shall be your territory. (Josh. 1:3–4)

Keep in mind, the Hebrews were gypsies. They didn't even own a sandlot. Yet in one grand, divine fiat, they were given the deed to the land of their dreams. God dangled the keys of Canaan in front of Moses' protégé and said, "Take it for a spin." And in one of Israel's finest moments, Joshua said, "Yes." He received his inheritance.

The word *inheritance* is to Joshua's book what delis are to Manhattan: everywhere. The word appears nearly sixty times. The command to possess the land is seen five times. The great accomplishment of the Hebrew people came down to this: "So Joshua let the people depart, each to his own inheritance" (Josh. 24:28).

Is it time for you to receive yours?

You have one. If you have given your heart to Christ, God has given Canaan to you. He "has blessed [you] with every spiritual blessing in the heavenly places in Christ" (Eph. 1:3).[4]

Note the tense: "he *has* blessed." Not "he *will* bless, *might* bless, or *someday could possibly* bless." No, the Promised Land property has been placed in your name. The courthouse records in heaven have been changed. God has already given you Canaan. You already have everything you need to be everything God desires. You have access to "every spiritual blessing in the heavenly places."

This well may be the best-kept secret in Christendom. We underestimate what happened to us upon conversion. As one writer observed, "Many Christians view their conversion as something like a car wash: You go in a filthy clunker; you come out with your sins washed away—a cleansed clunker."⁵ But conversion is more than a removal of sin. It is a deposit of power. It is as if your high-mileage, two-cylinder engine was extracted and a brand-new Ferrari engine was mounted in your frame. God removed the old motor, caked and cracked and broken with rebellion and evil, and replaced it with a humming, roaring version of himself. He embedded within you the essence of Christ. "Therefore, if anyone is in Christ, he is a new creation; old things have passed away; behold, all things have become new" (2 Cor. 5:17).

You are fully equipped! Need more energy? You have it. More kindness? It's yours. Could you use some self-control, self-discipline, or self-confidence? God will "equip you with all you need for doing his will" (Heb. 13:21 NLT). Just press the gas pedal. "God has given us everything we need for living a godly life" (2 Peter 1:3 NLT).

Glory Days begin with a paradigm shift.

In Canaan you do not fight *for* victory. You fight *from* victory. In the wilderness you strive. In Canaan you trust. In the wilderness you seek God's attention. In Canaan you already have God's favor. In the wilderness you doubt your salvation. In Canaan you know you are saved. You move from wanting-to-have to believing you already do.

When you were born into Christ, you were placed in God's royal family. "As many as received Him, to them He gave the right to become children of God" (John 1:12). Since you are a part of the family, you have access to the family blessings. All of them. "In Him also we have obtained an inheritance" (Eph. 1:11).

Surprised? You ain't heard nuttin' yet. In another passage the apostle Paul described the value of your portfolio. "The Spirit

Himself bears witness with our spirit that we are children of God, and if children, then heirs—heirs of God and joint heirs with Christ" (Rom. 8:16–17).

We are joint heirs with Christ. The Greek term in this passage is *sugkleronomos* (*sug*—together; *kleronomos*—inheritance).[6] We share the same inheritance as Christ! Our portion isn't a pittance. We don't inherit leftovers. We don't wear hand-me-downs. We aren't left out in the cold with the distant cousins. In the traditions of Paul's day, the firstborn son received a double portion while the rest of the siblings divvied up the remainder. Not so with Christ. "Our standing in the world is identical with Christ's" (1 John 4:17 MSG). Christ's portion is our portion! Whatever he has, we have!

Think what this means. Jesus cashed checks out of a boundless account. Grudges didn't corrode him. Despair didn't control him. Mood swings couldn't touch his joy. His conviction was bulletproof. He was the Fort Knox of faith. And when we give our hearts to him, he hands us his checkbook.

Then how do we explain the disconnect? If we are coheirs with Christ, why do we struggle through life? Our inheritance is perfect peace, yet we feel like a perfect mess. We have access to the joy level of Jesus yet plod along like dyspeptic donkeys. God promises to meet every need, yet we still worry and fret. Why?

I can think of a couple of reasons.

We don't know about our inheritance. No one ever told us about "the exceeding greatness of His power toward us who believe" (Eph. 1:19). No one ever told us that we fight from victory, not for victory. No one told us that the land is already conquered. Some Christians never live out of their inheritance because they don't know they have one.

But now you do. Now you know that you were made for more than the wilderness. God saved you from Egypt so that he could bless you in the Promised Land. Moses had to remind the people that "[God] brought us out from there, that He might bring us in [to Canaan]" (Deut. 6:23). There is a reason for our redemption too. God brought us out so he could lead us in. He set us free so he could raise us up.

The gift has been given. Will you trust it?

Ah, therein lies the second explanation for our weaknesses.

We don't believe in our inheritance. That was the problem of Joshua's ancestors. They didn't really believe that God could give them the land. The Glory Days of the Hebrews could have begun four decades earlier, a point God alluded to in his promise to Joshua: "Every place that the sole of your foot will tread upon I have given you, as I said to Moses" (Josh. 1:3). The reminder? *I made this offer to the people of Moses' day, but they didn't take it. They chose the wilderness. Don't make the same mistake.*

Joshua didn't. Much to his credit he took God at his word and set about the task of inheriting the land.

Do the same. Receive yours. You are embedded with the presence of God. Don't measure your life by your ability; measure it by God's. Even though you can't forgive, God can. And since he can, you can. You can't break the habit, but God can. Since he can, you can. You can't control your tongue, temper, or sexual urges, but God can. And since you have access to every blessing of heaven, you, in time, will find strength.

The car keys on the table are yours. The Promised Land life is yours for the taking. Make the mental shift from the wilderness to Canaan.

The wilderness mentality says, "I am weak, and I'll always be weak."

Canaan people say, "I was weak, but I am getting stronger."

Wilderness people say, "I'm a victim of my environment."

Promised Land people say, "I'm a victor in spite of my surroundings."

Wilderness people say, "These are difficult days. I'll never get through them."

God's people say, "These days are Glory Days. God will get me through."

Imagine what would happen if a generation of Christians lived out of their inheritance. Men and women would turn off Internet porn. The lonely would find comfort in God, not the arms of strangers. Struggling couples would spend more time in prayer, less time in anger. Children would consider it a blessing to care for their aging parents.

A generation of Christians would vacate the wilderness.

"God's power is very great for us who believe. That power is the same as the great strength God used to raise Christ from the dead" (Eph. 1:19–20 NCV).

The same steely, burly force that raised Christ from the dead will turn every "I can't" into "I can." "I can do all things through Christ, because he gives me strength" (Phil. 4:13 NCV).

A new day awaits you, my friend. A new season of accomplishment, discovery, and strength. Leave every "I can't" behind you. Set your "God can" ahead of you. Get ready to cross the Jordan.

3

TAKE HEED
TO THE VOICE
YOU HEED

Joshua 1:7–18

My dog ran away last week. (Dog lovers of the world, will you join me in a collective groan?)

A neighbor had tipped me off to a great place for dogs to romp and run. I told Andy, my dog, about it.

"Andy," I offered, "I know of a dog's dream come true. It is a creek bed with a wide meadow. No cars. No fences. No leashes. Just stuff to sniff and trees to wet and crevices to explore."

"Oh, Master Max," he barked, "you put the wow in *bowwow*. That sounds like the doggy version of Glory Days."

"Indeed it is. A canine Promised Land. But let me warn you. You must stay close to me. This pasture is several miles from our home. Deer will entice. Rabbits will lure. There may even be a seductive poodle on the path. You must stay alert. Heed my voice. Stay with me."

"I will," he yelped.

But did he? No. The moment I let him out of the car and unleashed him, he ran. He dashed through a grove of trees and scampered up a twenty-foot-tall bluff.

"Andy!" I shouted. He stopped and looked down at me.

He had a moral dilemma. On one side he heard the luring voices of the pasture. The wild life beckoned, "Come on, Andy. Let's have fun." On the other side he heard the voice of his wise, seasoned, and very handsome master. "Come here, Andy."

He looked my way. Then away. My way, then away. And then in a flash he was gone.

My first thought was *Denalyn is going to kill me.*

I ran after him, but he ran faster. "My next dog is going to be a basset hound," I resolved. My voice grew hoarse from yelling, and my legs grew weak from climbing. It took me forty-five minutes to find him. Finally there he was. Lying beneath a tree. Exhausted, thirsty, and, can I say, repentant.

"Go ahead," he offered. "Use me in your book. I entered the Promised Land, but I failed to listen to my master."

I wasn't intending to use my prodigal pup as an illustration, but since he offered, the story does fit the moment. God was concerned that Joshua and his people would forget their Master's instructions. Canaan was full of new, strange, alluring voices. Hence, the pre-Promised Land caution:

> Only be strong and very courageous, that you may observe to do according to all the law which Moses My servant commanded you; do not turn from it to the right hand or to the left, that you may prosper wherever you go. This Book of the Law shall not depart from your mouth, but you shall meditate in it day and night, that you may observe to do according to all that is written in it. For then you will make your way prosperous, and then you will have good success. (Josh. 1:7–8)

God was calling Joshua to lead two million ex-slaves into Canaan to inherit their inheritance. He was equipping the general for the mission of a lifetime. And what command did God give Joshua? Read the Word of God.

Like you and me, Joshua had a Bible. His Bible had five books— Genesis, Exodus, Leviticus, Numbers, and at least portions of Deuteronomy—which were carried alongside the ark of the covenant. But it wasn't enough for Joshua to possess the Scriptures; God wanted the Scriptures to possess Joshua. "This Book of the Law shall not depart from your mouth" (v. 8).

This was God's command to the commander of Israel. Though he was the unquestioned five-star general of the army, Joshua was subject to God's law. God did not tell him to create law or invent statutes but to be regulated by what was "written."

God didn't command Joshua to seek a spiritual experience, pursue a personal revelation, or long for goose bumps-giving emotion. God's word to him is his word to us: open the Bible.

The Bible is the most important tool in our spiritual growth. We can say this with confidence because of the good work of Greg Hawkins and Cally Parkinson. In the research for their book *Move*, they set out to find the key factors for spiritual growth. They asked the same question that we are asking: How do we move out of the wilderness into Canaan? Out of weak faith into life-giving faith?

Their study was conducted by an independent market-research firm. The secular company had no agenda other than to earn their fees by accurate analysis. They surveyed people in a thousand churches. And what they discovered raised the eyebrows of at least a thousand pastors.

> Nothing has a greater impact on spiritual growth than reflection on Scripture. If churches could do only one thing to help people at all levels of spiritual maturity grow in their relationship with Christ,

their choice is clear. They would inspire, encourage, and equip their people to read the Bible.[1]

The key to spiritual growth is not increased church attendance or involvement in spiritual activities. People don't grow in Christ because they are busy at church. They grow in Christ when they read and trust their Bibles.

Desire some Glory Days? Engage with the Bible. Meditate on it day and night. Think and rethink about God's Word. Let it be your guide. Make it your go-to book for questions. Let it be the ultimate authority in your life.

Don't chart your course according to the opinions of people or suggestions of culture. If you do, you will make the mistake that the farmer's son made. The father sent the boy to prepare a field, reminding him to till straight lines. "Select an object on the far side of the field, and plow straight at it."

Later when the father checked on the boy's progress, there wasn't a straight furrow to be found. Every row was uneven and wavy.

"I thought I told you to select an object and plow toward it," the dad said.

"I did," the boy answered, "but the rabbit kept hopping."

A straight line, like a good life, requires an unmoving target. Set your sights on the unchanging principles of God. Let God's Word be the authoritative word in your world.

This decision rubs against the skin of our culture. We prefer the authority of the voting booth, the pollster, or whatever feels good.

Such resistance is not novel with us. When Paul wrote a letter to Timothy, the apostle was helping the young pastor deal with the rage of selfishness in the culture. Paul listed nineteen characteristics of the people (2 Tim. 3:1–5), each of which was a fruit of rebellion. The way to deal with such self-absorption? Return to the Bible.

But you should continue following the teachings you learned. You know they are true, because you trust those who taught you. Since you were a child you have known the Holy Scriptures which are able to make you wise. And that wisdom leads to salvation through faith in Christ Jesus. All Scripture is inspired by God and is useful for teaching, for showing people what is wrong in their lives, for correcting faults, and for teaching how to live right. (2 Tim. 3:14–16 NCV)

According to Paul, the Bible exists to make us "wise for salvation through faith which is in Christ Jesus" (v. 15). We are lost and need to be saved. Jesus is our loving Savior and must be accepted. This is the primary message of Scripture.

But, we wonder, is the Bible really inspired? Can we believe Paul's assessment that "all Scripture is inspired by God"? Here is why I think we can.

It is remarkable in composition. Composed over sixteen centuries by forty authors. Written by soldiers, shepherds, farmers, and fishermen. Begun by Moses in Arabia and finished by John on Patmos. Penned by kings in palaces, shepherds in tents, and prisoners in prisons.

Would it be possible for forty writers, largely unknown to each other, writing in three different languages and several different countries, separated in time by as much as sixteen hundred years, to produce a book of singular theme unless behind them there was one mind and one designer?

It is remarkable in durability. It is the single most published book in history. Translated into at least twelve hundred languages by an army of translators.[2] It has outlived all its opponents. Bibles have been burned by governments and banished from courtrooms, but God's Word endures. The death knell has been sounded a hundred times, but God's Word continues.

It is remarkable in prophecy. Its pages contain more than three hundred fulfilled prophecies about the life of Christ,[3] yet they were all written at least four hundred years before he was born. What are the odds? Imagine if something similar occurred today. If we found a book written in the year 1900 that prophesied two world wars, a depression, an atomic bomb, and the assassinations of a president and a civil rights leader, wouldn't we trust it?

We also want to know if the Bible makes a difference. Does it work? Do the teachings of the Bible change us? There is only one way to find out. Click the Save button.

We all know what the Save button is. I do, and I am a remedial computer student. What great satisfaction occurs when, having created a document, we reach up and press the Save button.

The click reshapes the landscape of the hard drive. Words on the screen descend into the core of the machine. As long as the words are limited to the screen, they are vulnerable and exposed to the irascible cursor. It earns its name. We curse the little monster as it gobbles up our hard work. But once we save it, it is safe.

Are you clicking the button on Scripture? We save truth when we deliberately and consciously allow what we've heard to become a part of who we are. Jesus said, "You shall know the truth, and the truth shall make you free" (John 8:32). As we know (save) truth, the truth makes us free from guilt, fear, anger. Saved truth has a shaping, reconfiguring impact on a heart. Only when you allow the truth of Scripture to be the authority in your life can you know whether it works.

I have found this to be especially true in relationships. You may find this hard to believe, but not everyone likes the preacher. There are times when I misstep or misspeak and incur the displeasure of a parishioner. In the early years of my ministry, when I got wind of someone's unhappiness, I dismissed the problem. "If he doesn't bring it to me, then I have no hand in the matter."

But then I read Jesus' words: "If you bring your gift to the altar, and there remember that your brother has something against you, leave your gift there before the altar, and go your way. First be reconciled to your brother, and then come and offer your gift" (Matt. 5:23–24). Jesus commands the offender, even if unintentional, to take the initiative. I find that passage to be quite unpleasant.

Even so, I have tried to apply it to my fragile friendships.

"Bob," I have inquired, "have I said something to upset you?"

"Mary," I have asked, "there seems to be tension between us. Are we okay?"

Without fail the step has resulted in restoration. Never in my four decades of ministry has this practical teaching failed to achieve its goal. When Scripture is mixed with obedience, a healing elixir results.

God's Word works, but we must click the Save button.

The disciples of Jesus needed this reminder. On one occasion he told them, "Let us go over to the other side" (Mark 4:35 NIV). They did. En route to the other side of the Sea of Galilee, however, their boat encountered turbulence. "A furious squall came up, and the waves broke over the boat, so that it was nearly swamped" (v. 37 NIV). The sky opened, and buckets of water fell, and waves threatened to upend the boat. The disciples turned to Jesus and found him sound asleep! They screamed, "Don't you care if we drown?" (v. 38 NIV). Jesus woke up, stood up, commanded the storm to shut up, and then said to the disciples, "Do you still have no faith?" (v. 40 NIV).

What a stunning rebuke! The sea was raging; the water was churning. Why did Jesus scold them?

Simple. They didn't take him at his word. He said they were going to the other side. He didn't say, "We are going to the middle of the lake to drown." Jesus had declared the outcome. But when the storm came, the disciples heard the roar of the winds and forgot his word.

Storms are coming your way. Winds will howl, your boat will be tossed, and you will have a choice. Will you hear Christ or the crisis? Heed the promises of Scripture or the noise of the storm?

Glory Days require an ongoing trust in God's Word. Wilderness people trust Scripture just enough to escape Egypt. Canaan dwellers, on the other hand, make the Bible their go-to book for life.

As God told Joshua, "Meditate in it day and night" (Josh. 1:8). Literally, "you shall . . . mutter over this torah document."⁴ The image is one of a person reciting, rehearsing, reconsidering God's Word over and over again. Canaan is loud with enemy voices. The devil megaphones doubt and death into our ears. Take heed to the voice you heed.

"Let the word of Christ dwell in you richly in all wisdom, teaching and admonishing one another" (Col. 3:16). Chew it. Swallow it. Speak it.

Begin with a prayer. *God, please speak to my heart today as I read.* Then with an open heart read until a message hits you. I did this morning. I was reading in the book of Ephesians. Today's passage was a word to husbands to nourish and cherish their wives (5:28–29). I circled the two words on the page and prayed, *Lord, how can I nourish and cherish Denalyn?* The passage was in the back of my mind all day. Over lunch I even asked her. "Honey, how can I nourish you?" She looked at me as if I were speaking Russian. Still, I kept meditating.

Great rewards come to those who do. God promised Joshua, "You will make your way prosperous, and then you will have good success" (Josh. 1:8). This is the only place in the Old Testament where the two words *prosperous* and *success* are found together. This is an emphasized promise. Align yourself with God's Word and expect prosperity and success.

Don't cringe. Joshua 1:8 isn't a guarantee of early retirement. In the United States we often associate prosperity and success with money. The Bible is not so narrow. Its promise of prosperity *occasionally* includes money, but it far more often refers to a wealthy spirit, mind, and body. God prospers the leader with new skills, the worker with good sleep, the teacher with added patience, the mother with deeper affection, the elderly with greater hope. Scriptural fluency leads to spiritual affluence.

> Blessed is the man
> Who walks not in the counsel of the ungodly,
>> Nor stands in the path of sinners,
>> Nor sits in the seat of the scornful;
> But his delight is in the law of the LORD,
>> And in His law he meditates day and night.
> He shall be like a tree
>> Planted by the rivers of water,
>> That brings forth its fruit in its season,
>> Whose leaf also shall not wither;
> And whatever he does shall prosper. (Ps. 1:1–3)

God's command was enough for Joshua. He responded with direct obedience. He told his men, "Prepare provisions for yourselves, for within three days you will cross over this Jordan, to go in to possess the land which the LORD your God is giving you to possess" (Josh. 1:11).

No hesitation. No reservation. Unlike Sarah, who said, "I am too old" (see Gen. 18:12). Unlike Moses, who said, "I'm not a good speaker" (see Ex. 4:10). Unlike the disciples who said, "We don't have enough food to feed the hungry" (see Matt. 14:17). Others resisted God's call, but not Joshua. God said it. He believed it.

Do likewise. Learn a lesson from Joshua.

And learn a lesson from my dog, Andy. Knowing I would be writing this chapter, he spoke to me today.

"Master Max . . ."

(I love it when he calls me by that title.)

"Yes, Andy."

"Can you tell your readers something for me?"

"Of course."

"Tell them that I learned my lesson. Whenever I wander too far from my master's voice, my life is ruff, ruff, ruff."

4

IT'S OKAY IF YOU'RE NOT OKAY

Joshua 2

S ome kids in Cateura, on the outskirts of Asunción, Paraguay, are making music with their trash. They're turning washtubs into kettledrums and drainpipes into trumpets. Other orchestras fine-tune their maple cellos or brass tubas. Not this band. They play Beethoven sonatas with plastic buckets.

On their side of Asunción, garbage is the only crop to harvest. Garbage pickers sort and sell refuse for pennies a pound. Many of them have met the same fate as the trash; they've been tossed out and discarded.

But now, thanks to two men, they are making music.

Favio Chavez is an environmental technician who envisioned a music school as a welcome reprieve for the kids. Don Cola Gomez is a trash worker and carpenter. He had never seen, heard, or held a violin in his life. Yet when someone described the instrument, this untutored craftsman took a paint can and an oven tray into his tiny workshop and made a violin. His next instrument was a cello. He fashioned the body out of an oil barrel and made tuning knobs from a hairbrush, the heel of a shoe, and a wooden spoon.

Thanks to this Stradivarius, the junk gets a mulligan, and so do the kids who live among it. Since the day their story hit the news, they've been tutored by maestros, featured on national television programs, and on a world tour. They've been called the Landfill Harmonic and also the Recycled Orchestra of Cateura.[1]

We could also call them a picture of God's grace.

God makes music out of riffraff. Heaven's orchestra is composed of the unlikeliest of musicians. Peter, first-chair trumpeter, cursed the name of the Christ, who saved him. Paul plays the violin. But there was a day when he played the religious thug. And the guy on the harp? That's David. King David. Womanizing David. Conniving David. Bloodthirsty David. Repentant David.

Take special note of the woman with the clarinet. Her name is Rahab. Her story occupies the second chapter of Joshua. "Now Joshua the son of Nun sent out two men from Acacia Grove to spy secretly, saying, 'Go, view the land, especially Jericho.' So they went, and came to the house of a harlot named Rahab, and lodged there" (v. 1).

The time had come for the Hebrew people to enter the Promised Land. Jericho, a formidable town that sat just north of the Dead Sea, was their first challenge. Canaanites indwelled the city. To call the people barbaric is to describe the North Pole as nippy. These people turned temple worship into orgies. They buried babies alive. The people of Jericho had no regard for human life or respect for God.

It was into this city that the two spies of Joshua crept.

It was in this city that the spies met Rahab, the harlot.

Much could be said about Rahab without mentioning her profession. She was a Canaanite. She provided cover for the spies of Joshua. She came to believe in the God of Abraham before she ever met the children of Abraham. She was spared in the destruction of her city. She was grafted into the Hebrew culture. She married a contemporary of Joshua's, bore a son named Boaz, had a great-grandson named Jesse, a great-great-grandson named David, and a descendant named Jesus. Yes, Rahab's name appears on the family tree of the Son of God.

Her résumé needn't mention her profession. Yet in five of the eight appearances of her name in Scripture, she is presented as a "harlot."[2] Five! Wouldn't one suffice? And couldn't that one reference be nuanced in a euphemism such as "Rahab, the best *hostess* in Jericho" or "Rahab, who made everyone feel welcome"? It's bad enough that the name Rahab sounds like "rehab." Disguise her career choice. Veil it. Mask it. Put a little concealer on this biblical blemish. Drop the reference to the brothel, please.

But the Bible doesn't. Just the opposite. It points a neon sign at it. It's even attached to her name in the book of Hebrews Hall of Fame. The list includes Abel, Noah, Abraham, Isaac, Jacob, Joseph, Moses . . . and then, all of a sudden, "the harlot Rahab" (11:31). No asterisk, no footnote, no apology. Her history of harlotry is part of her testimony.

Her story begins like this: "And it was told the king of Jericho, saying, 'Behold, men have come here tonight from the children of Israel to search out the country'" (Josh. 2:2). The king could see the multitude of Hebrews camped on Jordan's eastern banks. As Rahab would later disclose, the people of Jericho were scared. Word on the street was that God had his hand on the newcomers and woe be unto anyone who got in their way. When the king heard that the spies were hiding at Rahab's house, he sent soldiers to fetch them.

I'm seeing half a dozen men squeeze down the narrow cobblestoned path in the red-light district. It's late at night. The torch-lit taverns are open, and the patrons are a few sheets to the wind. They yell obscenities at the king's men, but the soldiers don't react. The guards keep walking until they stand before the wooden door of a stone building that abuts the famous Jericho walls. The lantern is unlit, leaving the soldiers to wonder if anyone is home. The captain pounds on the door. There is a shuffling inside. Rahab answers. Her makeup is layered and her eyes are shadowed. Her low-cut robe reveals the fringe of a lacy secret that Victoria couldn't keep. Her voice is husky from one cigarette too many. She positions one hand on her hip and holds a dirty martini with the other.

"Sorry, boys, we're booked for the night."

"We aren't here for that," the captain snaps. "We're here for the Hebrews."

"Hebrews?" She cocks her head. "I thought you were here for fun."

She winks an eyelid, heavy with mascara, at a young soldier. He blushes, but the captain stays focused.

"We came for the spies. Where are they?"

She steps out onto the porch, looks to the right and left, and then lowers her voice to a whisper. "You just missed them. They snuck out before the gates were shut. If you get a move on, you can catch them."

The king's men turn and run. As they disappear around the corner, Rahab hurries up the brothel stairs to the roof, where the two spies have been hiding. She tells them the coast is clear. "The whole city is talking about you and your armies. Everyone is freaking out. The king can't sleep, and the people can't eat. They're popping Xanax like Tic Tacs. The last ounce of courage left on the morning train." (I'm using the LPV—Lucado Paraphrase Version.)

Her words must have stunned the spies. They never expected to find cowards in Jericho. And, even more, they never expected to find faith in a brothel. But they did. Read what Jericho's shady lady said to them:

> I know that the LORD has given you the land . . . [W]e have heard how
> the LORD dried up the water of the Red Sea . . . and what you did to

the two kings . . . who were on the other side of the Jordan . . . [T]he LORD your God, He is God in heaven above and on earth beneath. (vv. 9–11)

Well, what do you know? Rahab found God. Or, better worded, God found Rahab. He spotted a tender heart in this hard city and reached out to save her. He would have saved the entire city, but no one else made the request. Then again, Rahab had an advantage over the other people. She had nothing to lose. She was at the bottom of the rung. She'd already lost her reputation, her social standing, her chance for advancement. She was at the bottom of the pit.

Perhaps that is where you are as well.

You may or may not sell your body, but you've sold your allegiance, affection, attention, and talents. You've sold out. We all have. We've wondered, we've all wondered, *Glory Days? Perhaps for him or for her. But not for me. I am too . . . soiled, dirty, afflicted. I have sinned too much, stumbled too often, floundered too long. I'm on the garbage heap of society. No Glory Days for me.*

God's one-word reply for such doubt? *Rahab*!

Lest we think God's Promised Land is promised to a chosen few, he positions her story in the front of the book. The narrator gives her an entire chapter, for heaven's sake! She gets more inches of type than do the priests, the spies, or Joshua's right-hand man. If quantity and chronology mean anything in theology, then Rahab's headline position announces this: God has a place for the Rahabs of the world.

As evidence, consider Rahab's New Testament counterpart, the Samaritan woman. By the time Jesus met her, she was on a first-century version of a downward spiral. Five ex-husbands and half a dozen kids, each looking like a different daddy. Decades of loose living had left her tattooed and tabooed and living with a boyfriend who thought a wedding was a waste of time.

Gossipers wagged their tongues about her. How else can we explain her midday appearance at the water well? Other women filled their buckets at sunrise, but this woman opted for noon, preferring, I suppose, the heat of the sun over the heat of their scorn.

Were it not for the appearance of a Stranger, her story would have been lost in the Samaritan sands. But he entered her life with a promise of endless water and quenched thirst. He wasn't put off by her past. Just the opposite. He offered to make music out of her garbage. She accepted his offer. We know because of what happened next.

Many Samaritans from the village believed in Jesus because the woman had said, "He told me everything I ever did!" When they came out to see him, they begged him to stay in their village. So he stayed for two days, long enough for many more to hear his message and believe. Then they said to the woman, "Now we believe, not just because of what you told us, but because we have heard him ourselves. Now we know that he is indeed the Savior of the world." (John 4:39–42 NLT)

The woman on the margin became the woman with the message. No one else gave her a chance. Jesus gave her the chance of a lifetime. He came for people like her.

For people like the women of Grace House. Grace House is a transition home for women who are coming out of prison. They live under the same roof, eat at the same table, and seek the same Lord. They study the Bible. They learn a trade. Most of all, they learn to trust their new identity.

I recently attended a fund-raiser for the ministry. One of the residents gave her testimony at the dinner. She described a life of prostitution, drugs, and alcohol. She lost her marriage, her children, and ultimately her freedom. But then Christ found her. What struck me was the repeated rhythm of her story: "I was . . . but now . . ." "I was on drugs, but now I'm clean." "I was on the streets, but now I'm on my feet."

I was . . . but now . . . This is the chorus of grace. And this is the work of God. And what a work he did in the life of Rahab.

The Hebrew spies, as it turns out, were actually missionaries. They thought they were on a reconnaissance trip. They weren't. God needed no scouting report. His plan was to collapse the city walls like a stack of dominoes. He didn't send the men to collect data. He sent the spies to reach Rahab. They told her to "bind this line of scarlet cord in the window" so they could identify her house (Josh. 2:18). Without hesitation she bound the scarlet cord in the window.

The spies escaped and Rahab made preparation. She told her family to get ready. She kept an eye out for the coming army. She checked (don't you know she checked!) the cord to make sure it was tied securely and dangling from the window.

When the Hebrews came and the walls fell, when everyone else perished, Rahab and her family were saved. "By faith the harlot Rahab did not perish" (Heb. 11:31). Her profession of faith mattered more than her profession as a harlot.

Maybe your past is a checkered one.

Maybe your peers don't share your faith.

Maybe your pedigree is one of violence, your ancestry one of rebellion.

If so, then Rahab is your model.

We don't drop scarlet cords from our windows. But we trust the crimson thread of Christ's blood. We don't prepare for the coming of the Hebrews, but we do live with an eye toward the second coming of our Joshua—Jesus Christ.

Ultimately we will all see what the people of Asunción are discovering. Our mess will become music, and God will have a heaven full of rescued Rahabs in his symphony. That'll be me on the tuba. And you? What will you be playing? One thing is for sure. We will all know "Amazing Grace" by heart.

5

UNPACK
YOUR BAGS

Joshua 3

Jimmy Wayne never knew his father. His mom spent more time in prison than out. When he was twelve years old, she was released from jail and took up with a troublemaker. They loaded Jimmy into the backseat of the Olds Delta 88, and for a year the car was his home. "It had bench seats and smelled like body odor," remembers Jimmy. They drove from city to city, avoiding the police.

After miles of drifting they dumped Jimmy in the parking lot of a Pensacola, Florida, bus station and drove off. He was thirteen years old. He had no home. No future. No provision. One day while wandering through a neighborhood, he spotted an older man who was at work in a garage wood shop.

He approached the elderly gentleman and asked if the man had any work. The carpenter sized up the boy, assessed him to be homeless, and decided to give him a chance. The man introduced himself as Russell. He called for his wife, Bea, to come to the garage. They showed Jimmy the lawn mower and how to operate it.

For several weeks Jimmy cut the couple's grass and survived on the twenty dollars they paid him each week. After some time Bea asked Jimmy where he lived. At first he lied, afraid she wouldn't let a homeless boy work. But finally she convinced him to tell her the truth. When he did, the couple took him in.

They gave him his own bedroom, bathroom, and place at the dinner table. The home was like heaven to Jimmy. He took a hot bath and ate hot meals. He even sat with the family in the living room and watched television in the evening. Still, in spite of their kindness, Jimmy refused to unpack his bag. He'd been turned away so many times that he'd learned to be wary. For four days his plastic bag sat on the floor, full of clothes, ready to be snatched up when Bea and Russell changed their minds.

He was in the house but not *in* the house. He was under the roof but not under the promise. He was with the family but didn't behave like a family member.

Russell eventually convinced Jimmy to unpack and move in. It took several days, a dozen or so meals, and more than one heart-to-heart conversation. But Russell persuaded Jimmy to trust them to care for him.[1]

Our Father is still working to convince us.

Maybe you question your place in God's family. You fear his impending rejection. You wrestle with doubt-laced questions: Am I really in God's family? What if God changes his mind? Reverses his acceptance? Lord knows, he has reason to do so. We press forward only to fall back. We renew our resolve only to stumble again. We wonder, *Will God turn me out?*

Boyfriends do. Employers do. Coaches kick players off the team. Teachers expel students from school. Parents give birth to children and abandon them at bus stations. How do we know God won't do the same? What if he changes his mind about us? After all, he is holy and pure, and we are anything but. Is it safe to unpack our bags?

God answered this question at the cross. When Jesus died, the heavenly vote was forever cast in your favor and mine. He declared for all to hear, "This child is my child. My covenant will never change."

Promised Land people believe this. They trust God's hold on them more than their hold on God. They place their trust in the finished work of Christ. They deeply believe that they are "delivered . . . from the power of darkness and conveyed . . . into the kingdom of the Son" (Col. 1:13). They know that Jesus was serious when he said, "[My children] shall never perish; no one will snatch them out of my hand" (John 10:28 NIV).

They point to Calvary as prima facie evidence of God's commitment to them.

The followers of Joshua did something similar. They looked not to a hill but to a river. Not to Calvary but to the Jordan. The miraculous crossing convinced them that God was in their presence. As their leader had promised, "By this [crossing] you shall know that the living God is among you" (v. 10).

During most months of the year, the Jordan was thirty or forty yards wide, maybe six feet deep.[2] But Joshua received his orders during the season of harvest (3:15). The Jordan swelled to a mile in width, turbulent with the melted snows of Mount Hermon. Crossing the swollen current was no small task.

Especially with millions of people! "Go over this Jordan, you and all this people" (Josh. 1:2). God wanted every man, woman, child, and infant across the river. Not just the hearty and healthy, but the old and feeble, sick and disabled. No one would be left behind. Joshua might well have gulped at this command. Two million people crossing a mile-wide river?

Yet he set the process in motion. "Joshua rose early in the morning; and they set out from Acacia Grove and came to the Jordan, he and all the children of Israel, and lodged there before they crossed over" (3:1).

The people pitched their tents on the eastern edge of the river. For three days they waited, watching the copper-colored waters and yeasty waves carry debris and trunks of trees. For three nights they slept, or tried to sleep, listening to the endless rush of water in the dark.

Three days. Plenty of time to ask plenty of questions. How will we get across? Will we use a boat? Will someone build a bridge? Will everyone really go? What about the frail? What about the children? Most of all, how can a nation of people cross a flooded, bridgeless, boatless river?

On the third day the answer came.

> Officers went through the camp; and they commanded the people, saying, "When you see the ark of the covenant of the LORD your God, and the priests, the Levites, bearing it, then you shall set out from your place and go after it." (vv. 2–3)

The ark of the covenant was a small rectangular box, commissioned by God, that contained a trio of Hebrew artifacts: unspoiled manna, Aaron's walking stick, and the precious stone tablets that had felt the engraving finger of God. A heavy golden plate, called the mercy seat, served as a lid to the chest. Two gold cherubim with outstretched wings faced each other and looked down on the golden lid. The dwelling place of God was between the angels.

When God said, "Follow the ark," he was saying, "Follow me."

God led the way. Not soldiers. Not Joshua. Not engineers and their plans or Special Forces and their equipment. When it came time to pass through the impassable waters, God's plan was simple: trust me.

The people did. At the close of the three days, there was a stirring in the Hebrew camp. A chosen band of priests, robed in white, walked toward the river. They carried the ark with acacia poles that ran through corner rings and sat on their shoulders. People stepped out of their tents and watched in hushed silence as priests inched their way down the terraced bank toward the Jordan. The only sound was the rush of the water.

It showed no sign of stopping. When they were thirty feet from the riverbank, the Jordan was still a rushing current. Twenty feet, ten feet, five feet. Fast and furious. Even when the priests were a single step from the water, the flow did not slow. Surely the men paused. Should they proceed? The white-capped flood would knock them over and take the ark with it. Then they remembered what Joshua had said: "When you have come to the edge of the water of the Jordan, you shall stand in the Jordan" (v. 8).

Scripture does not veil their fear: "As those who bore the ark came to the Jordan, and the feet of the priests who bore the ark dipped in the edge of the water . . ." (v. 15). The priests "dipped" their feet into the edge of the water. They did not run, plunge, or dive into the river. They placed ever so carefully the tips of their big toes in the river. It was the smallest of steps, but with God the smallest step of faith can activate the mightiest of miracles. As they touched the water, the flow stopped as if someone had shut off the water main. "The waters which came down from upstream stood still, and rose in a heap very far away at Adam, the city that is beside Zaretan" (v. 16).

Zaretan was thirty miles upriver. Thirty miles! In my imagination I had always envisioned a wall of water forming to the side of the ark and the priests. Not so. God began his work upriver. He wanted a wide path through which two million people could cross en masse.

And cross they did! "All Israel crossed over on dry ground, until all the people had crossed completely over the Jordan" (v. 17).

"*All Israel* crossed over on dry ground." The men. The women. Old. Young. Feeble. Forceful. Believers and doubters. The faithful and the murmurers.

"All Israel crossed over *on dry ground.*" Might as well have been concrete. No wagon wheels got stuck. No feet got damp. As the people stood on the western shore, they had no mud on their sandals, no water on their robes, and, most of all, no fear in their hearts.

God did for them what they could not do. Imagine the Israelites as they stood on the western banks of the Jordan. High fives and shouts of "Man alive!" all around!

Did they not brim with confidence? Did they not stand in awe of God? If God could turn a raging river into a red carpet, then "Watch out, Jericho. Here we come!" As Joshua had told them, "By this [crossing] you shall know that the living God is among you" (3:10). The Hebrews knew they couldn't lose! The bicycle race was downhill with the wind at their backs. They had every right to celebrate.

So do we.

For Joshua's people, assurance came as they stood on dry land looking back at the Jordan.

For us, assurance comes as we stand on the finished work of Christ and look back at the cross.

The river we could not cross? Jesus crossed it. The tide we could not face? He faced it. For us. All of us! The young, the old. The courageous, the timid. Our deliverance is complete.

Like the Hebrews we have been dramatically delivered.

But are we deeply convinced?

Remember, the Hebrews could have entered Canaan four decades earlier. The prior generation had experienced a miracle every bit as grand. They had crossed the Red Sea (Ex. 14:21–22). Both crossings involved large bodies of water and passage over dry ground. The difference between the first crossing and the second? Joshua's generation paid attention. The Jordan River crossing convinced them that God was with them.

Let the cross convince you. Be settled about God's faithfulness.

In one of the psalms the writer described a person of faith with these words: "He is settled in his mind that Jehovah will take care of him" (Ps. 112:7 TLB). Life has many unanswered questions, but God's ability to save needn't be one of them. Let this issue be settled once and for all.

Look at you. There is no mud on your sandals, no water on your robe. There is no sin on your record, no guilt attached to your name. Let there be no doubt in your heart. If God "did not spare his own Son but gave him for us all," will he not also give you all you need for a Promised Land life (Rom. 8:32 NCV)?

Join the chorus of the confident and declare, "I am convinced that nothing can ever separate us from God's love . . . [I]ndeed, nothing in all creation will ever be able to separate us from the love of God that is revealed in Christ Jesus our Lord" (vv. 38–39 NLT).

Rest in your redemption. The past is past. The future is bright. God's Word is sure. His work is finished. You are a covenant partner with God, a full-fledged member of his Promised Land development program.

The Jordan is behind you.

Canaan is before you.

A new season awaits you.

Jimmy Wayne found a new season. He took his place in the family. He went on to get an education. He found a career as a country music singer and songwriter.

His best days began when he unpacked his bags. Yours will too.

6

DON'T FORGET
TO REMEMBER

Joshua 4:1–5:12

For a book about conquests Joshua sure skimps on military details. What weapons did Joshua's army use? How many officers did his army have? How many men made up each battalion? Did Joshua have an elite force? If so, what training did he require? The answer to these and other questions?

We don't know.

We don't know because the emphasis is not on a physical battle but a spiritual one. The real conflict wasn't with Canaanites or Amorites; it was with Satan and his demons.

Canaan was the choicest real estate on earth. It connected Africa with Europe. It accessed the Mediterranean Sea. It was marked by fertile fields and valleys. Most important, the land was God's gift to Israel. Nearly seven centuries earlier God had told Abram, "To your descendants I will give this land" (Gen. 12:7).

God set this property apart for his people and his people apart to be a blessing for the world. God promised Abram, "I will make you a great nation; I will bless you and make your name great; and you shall be a blessing" (v. 2). The Hebrews were the couriers of God's covenant to a galaxy of people. Israel was the parchment on which God's redemption story would be written. The city of Jerusalem. The town of Bethlehem. The sacrifices of the temple. The prophecies of the prophets. All on this land.

The Redeemer would be born here, walk here, and live his life here. He would soak this dirt with his blood and shake this ground with his resurrection. The book of Joshua isn't about claiming real estate for a dislocated nation. It is about preserving a stage for God's redemption plan.

Satan's counterstrategy was clear: contaminate the Promised Land and preempt the promised Child. Destroy God's people and destroy God's work.

Joshua's battle, then, was a spiritual one.

So is ours.

> Our fight is not against people on earth but against the rulers and authorities and the powers of this world's darkness, against the spiritual powers of evil in the heavenly world. That is why you need to put on God's full armor. Then on the day of evil you will be able to stand strong. And when you have finished the whole fight, you will still be standing. So stand strong, with the belt of truth tied around your waist and the protection of right living on your chest. On your feet wear the Good News of peace to help you stand strong. And also use the shield of faith with which you can stop all the burning arrows of the Evil One. (Eph. 6:12–16 NCV)

The idea of an actual devil strikes many people as odd and out-dated. The popular trend of our day is to blame problems on genetics, governments, and environments. Yet the Bible presents a real and present foe of our faith. His name is Satan. Some call him the devil. Others call him Beelzebub, Belial, the obstructor, the tempter, the evil one, the accuser, the prince of demons, the ruler of this world, or the prince of the power of the air. Whatever name you choose, he is the enemy, and he is real.

He is not the cute and harmless character of the cartoons. He is not an imaginary, dark counterpart to the Easter Bunny. He is the invisible yet forceful fallen angel called Lucifer, who desired the high place only God could occupy. He rebelled and disobeyed and wants you and me to do the same. "The devil, your enemy, goes around like a roaring lion looking for someone to eat" (1 Peter 5:8 NCV).

Any person who has dared to draw near to God has felt Satan's attack.

Want to read his rap sheet?

"Satan . . . incited David" (1 Chron. 21:1 NIV).

"Satan has asked . . . to sift you [Simon] like wheat" (Luke 22:31 TLB).

"The devil . . . persuaded Judas Iscariot . . . to turn against Jesus" (John 13:2 NCV).

"This woman . . . Satan has kept bound for eighteen long years" (Luke 13:16 NIV).

He has "blinded the minds of those who don't believe. As a result, they don't see the light of the Good News" (2 Cor. 4:4 GOD'S WORD).

"He rules the world, and his spirit has power over everyone who doesn't obey God" (Eph. 2:2 CEV).

Satan incites, sifts, persuades, binds, blinds, and rules.

He has one objective: "to steal, and to kill, and to destroy" (John 10:10).

He's ticked off at you. All this talk about Glory Days and Promised Land living has him in a foul mood. Your wilderness days did not trouble him. But now you are stepping into your Promised Land life. Daring to walk in faith, not fear; leaning on grace, not guilt; hearing God's voice more, the devil's voice less.

Consequently, Satan's got you in his sights. You are in enemy territory.

Joshua was. For the first time in nearly five centuries, Hebrews were camping in Canaan. This was the moment they had been waiting for. How many times had they gazed across the Jordan at the lush land? Some of them, like Joshua and Caleb, had been waiting for forty years! When God opened the waters of the Jordan River, they didn't wait to be asked twice. "All told, about forty thousand armed soldiers crossed over before GOD to the plains of Jericho, ready for battle" (Josh. 4:13 MSG). They hurried across with a shout, a whoop, and a holler. Had God not stopped them, they would have run straight to Jericho.

But God did stop them. They weren't quite ready. It's as if he wanted to give them one more word.

I'm picturing the mom who is sending her child off to school for the first time. The backpack is full. Breakfast has been eaten. The bus is waiting. Little Junior is so excited to get out the door. But Mommy stops him on the porch. She lowers herself to be eye level with her son and says, "Remember what I have taught you. Remember who you are. Remember whose you are."

God did this. He brought the invasion to a halt, and by virtue of two commands he prepared the Hebrews for the Promised Land.

> And it came to pass, when all the people had completely crossed over the Jordan, that the LORD spoke to Joshua, saying: "Take for yourselves twelve men from the people, one man from every tribe, and command them, saying, 'Take for yourselves twelve stones from here, out of the midst of the Jordan, from the place where the priests' feet stood firm. You shall carry them over with you and leave them in the lodging place where you lodge tonight.'" (vv. 1–3)

Joshua commanded a dozen men, one from each tribe, to return to the riverbed. From the very area where the priests had stood, the men dislodged twelve rocks. As the people watched and the waters resumed their flow, Joshua stacked the stones. When the twelfth rock was securely placed on the top spot, he turned to his people and urged, "When your children ask their fathers in time to come, saying, 'What are these stones?' then you shall let your children know, saying, 'Israel crossed over this Jordan on dry land'; for the LORD your God dried up the waters of the Jordan before you until you had crossed over" (vv. 21–23).

The secret of survival in enemy territory? *Remember . . .*

Remember what God has done. Record his accomplishments in your memoirs. Capture this crossing in your memory. Before you look forward to Jericho, look backward to Jordan and what God accomplished there.

Some years back my daughter Andrea reminded me of this truth. As I was driving her to middle school one morning, she noticed that I was anxious.

"Why are you so quiet, Dad?"

I told her that I was worried about meeting a book deadline.

Kids aren't always clued in on their father's profession, so she asked me, "Haven't you written other books?"

"Yes."

"How many?"

At that point the answer was fifteen.

"Have you ever missed a deadline before?"

"No."

"So God has helped you fifteen times already?"

"Yes."

"He's helped you each time?"

I winced. She was sounding like her mother.

"If he has helped you fifteen different times, don't you think he will help you this time?"

Translation: stack some stones, Dad.

Satan has no recourse to your testimony. Your best weapon against his attacks is a good memory.

Don't forget a single blessing!

He forgives your sins—every one.
    He heals your diseases—every one.
    He redeems you from hell—saves your life!
    He crowns you with love and mercy—a paradise crown.
    He wraps you in goodness—beauty eternal.
    He renews your youth—you're always young in his presence.

GOD makes everything come out right;
    he puts victims back on their feet. (Ps. 103:2–6 MSG)

Create a trophy room in your heart. Each time you experience a victory, place a memory on the shelf. Before you face a challenge, take a quick tour of God's accomplishments. Look at all the paychecks he has provided, all the blessings he has given, all the prayers he has answered. Imitate the shepherd boy David. Before he fought Goliath, the giant, he remembered how God had helped him kill a lion and a bear (1 Sam. 17:34–36). He faced his future by revisiting the past. Don't go to Jericho until you've remembered Jordan.

"Okay, okay," I'm imagining an impatient soldier saying. "The stones are stacked, and the moment is memorialized. Can we attack now?"

Not quite. God had one more instruction for the Hebrews before sending them into battle: *Remember whose you are.*

At that time the LORD said to Joshua, "Make flint knives for yourself, and circumcise the sons of Israel again the second time." (Josh. 5:2)

Six hundred years earlier God had inaugurated the practice of male circumcision. "[Circumcision]," he told Abraham, "shall be a sign of the covenant between Me and you" (Gen. 17:11). Eight days after birth every male child was to be symbolically set apart, his organ of male identity altered. He was not like the pagans, who didn't know God. He was a child of the covenant. He belonged to God.

During the wilderness wanderings the Hebrews let this practice lapse. It's not hard to see why. With hearts hardened the people ignored the instructions.

They might have been tempted to ignore them again. The act would leave the men convalescing for weeks. Their wives and children would be unprotected. Enemy nations were watching their every move. Shouldn't the men remain at maximum strength so they could fight?

Yet God was not concerned with their numbers, skills, or muscles. He wanted them to remember whose they were. Specifically, he "rolled away the reproach of Egypt" (Josh. 5:9). The "reproach of Egypt" was the humiliation of slavery that had made them subject to insult and disgrace from other nations. It was time to reclaim their birthright as God's chosen people.

Circumcision, then, was also a symbolic separation from the past. The act declared a new identity. "You are no longer who you were. You are mine." No longer slaves but free. No longer in bondage but liberated.

God's message to the Hebrews? Remember whose you are.

God's message to us? Remember whose you are.

In a sense all believers have been circumcised. This may be news to you. "When you came to Christ, he set you free from your evil desires, not by a bodily operation of circumcision but by a spiritual operation, the baptism of your souls" (Col. 2:11 TLB).

Christ cut away the old life. He severed from you the power of sin and death. The old temptations, lusts, and longings? He detached you from their power when you gave your heart to Christ. It cannot be stated too often or too clearly. You are not the person you used to be. Your former self no longer exists. The old life is disempowered. When Christ died, you died. When Christ was buried, you were buried. When Christ rose from the dead, you arose with him. You are a new you. You can "put off . . . the old man" and "put on the new" (Eph. 4:22, 24). Who is the new you?

I'm glad you asked.

You are

God's child (John 1:12),
Christ's friend (John 15:15),
a member of Christ's body (1 Cor. 12:27),
a saint (Eph. 1:1),
redeemed and forgiven of all your sins (Col. 1:14),
complete in Christ, lacking in nothing (Col. 2:10),
free from condemnation (Rom. 8:1–2),
God's coworker (2 Cor. 6:1),
seated with Christ in the heavenly realm (Eph. 2:6),
God's workmanship (Eph. 2:10),
a citizen of heaven (Phil. 3:20),
adopted into God's family (Eph. 1:5),
born of God, and the evil one cannot touch you (1 John 5:18).

Get acquainted with your new self. "Consider yourselves to be dead to the power of sin and alive to God" (Rom. 6:11 NLT). When the devil draws near, stand against him. "What are you doing here?

I am dead to you!" Give him no quarter. Don't take his lies. Don't stand for his accusations. Don't cower at his attacks. When he dredges up your past mistakes, tell him whose you are. He has no recourse to this truth. He knows who you are. He just hopes that you don't or that you will forget. So prove to him that you know and remember. Tell him:

"I have been bought with a price. I belong to God" (see 1 Cor. 6:20).

"I have not been given a spirit of fear but of power, love, and a sound mind" (see 2 Tim. 1:7).

"I cannot be separated from the love of God" (see Rom. 8:35).

"I can find grace and mercy at the time of need" (see Heb. 4:16).

"I can do all things through Christ who strengthens me" (Phil. 4:13).

Promised Land people think like this. They walk with a reverent swagger. They live out of their inheritance. They show the devil the new name on their spiritual passport.

They are spiritually circumcised. I know that term sounds terribly awkward and indelicate. But it is a biblical concept. You are a new creation. "God's Spirit, who is in you, is greater than the devil, who is in the world" (1 John 4:4 NCV).

The secret of survival in enemy territory? Remember. Remember what God has done. Remember whose you are.

The Hebrews did what God commanded—and God protected them.

> So it was, when all the kings of the Amorites who were on the west side of the Jordan, and all the kings of the Canaanites who were by the sea, heard that the LORD had dried up the waters of the Jordan . . . their heart melted; and there was no spirit in them any longer because of the children of Israel. (Josh. 5:1)

Devotion prompted divine protection.

Don't face Satan by facing Satan. Face Satan by facing God.

Don't obsess yourself with the devil. No need to master in the hierarchy of hell. No need to disentangle the puzzle of principalities. Don't give Old Scratch the time of day. Glance at the devil and gaze at Christ.

Yes, it is a war out there. But the war is already won. "God stripped the spiritual rulers and powers of their authority. With the cross, he won the victory and showed the world that they were powerless" (Col. 2:15 NCV).

Satan is a fallen angel whose time is short.

Don't let him mess with your Glory Days. Neutralize him.

Remember what God has done. Face the future by remembering the past.

Remember whose you are. You are not who you used to be. You are God's child.

Then, and only then, will you be ready to face Jericho.

7

CALL ON YOUR COMMANDER

Joshua 5:13–15

J oy Veron was all alone in her hospital room. Alone with her fears, her pain, and her memory of the SUV rolling over her body. Vacation became tragedy when her car slipped out of gear and began rolling toward a steep Colorado mountain ravine, carrying her three children. Joy and her parents were looking at a cabin her parents were considering buying. When they saw the vehicle moving, they dashed to stop it. Joy arrived first. Fearful she didn't have time to open the driver's side door, she placed herself in front of the SUV. Her interference slowed it down enough for her father to climb in from the passenger side and bring the car to a stop. That was October of 1999. Her children still remember the expression on her face as the car pulled her under.

Joy's back was broken, and the internal damage was severe.

Joy was airlifted to a hospital in Farmington, New Mexico. Her condition was so fragile the doctors waited twelve days before doing surgery. She emerged from the operation with a dangerously high fever. Her medical team struggled to get the fever under control but couldn't. For seven days her temperature raged. So did her fears. She feared dying. Then she feared living as a paralytic. The physicians tried to comfort her, but there was no comfort to be had. Joy pleaded with her mom for help. Her mother, who had maintained a bedside vigil, stepped out to call friends for prayer.

"I'll be back soon," she told her daughter.

Joy was all alone. But not for long. A man opened the door and walked into the room. Joy did not recognize him. All her nurses, per her request, were females. If the man was a doctor, he wasn't one of hers. He had a striking appearance, tall and dressed in white. He had high cheekbones and silver-white hair that was parted in the middle and ran down his back in a ponytail. And his eyes . . . oh, his eyes! Fourteen years later as Joy described them to me, her face lit up. "They were crystal blue and bright." She smiled. "I've never seen such beautiful eyes."

The visitor stepped toward her bed and lifted her chart. He casually flipped through the pages, but Joy had the impression that he was not reading them. After a few moments he spoke to her with a soothing voice. "Joy, you are going to be all right. You will get through this."

He looked at her, and then as quickly as he had entered, he left.

Joy instantly believed him. "Had the doctor, a nurse, or a family member said those words, I would have doubted them. But when this stranger spoke, there was a knowing in my inner person. He knew me. And I believed him. I knew I was going to be okay."

When her mother reentered the room, Joy immediately told her about the man. "Mom, he said I am going to be fine!"

Joy's mom ran out into the hall to find the visitor but saw no one matching his description. She described him to the staff. They knew nothing of such a man. They searched the hospital. They could not find him.

Joy knows why. She believes the visitor was heaven-sent just for her. She treasures the words he spoke. The years have brought pain, difficulty, and a life in a wheelchair. Joy often turns to the memory of the blue-eyed guest for strength.

"You are going to be all right. You will get through this."

And she has.[1]

Who was this visitor? From where did he come? Did God send an emissary to bring her hope?

Joshua would like to weigh in on this discussion. He has a story that parallels Joy's, a divine encounter during a dark, difficult time. He wasn't alone in a hospital, but he was alone with a challenge. "Joshua was near Jericho" (Josh. 5:13 NIV).

David had his Goliath. Elijah had his Jezebel. John had the Roman Empire. And Joshua had the people of this fortified city. It towered like a titan on the barren plains north of the Dead Sea. Successive walls encircled the stone houses.[2] The outer wall was seven feet wide and sixteen feet high. On top of this wall a second wall was built, this one eight feet tall. A citadel guarded the north end. A thick forest of palm trees, eight miles long and three miles wide, stood as a barrier east of the city. Steep hills protected the western wall.[3]

High walls. Protected sides. Joshua and his soldiers had never faced such a challenge. They had fought battles in the wilderness but always on their turf and terms on an open plain. Never, ever had they fought a fortified city. They had never passed this way before.

Perhaps you haven't either.

Perhaps you are facing a challenge unlike any you have ever faced before. It looms on the horizon like an angry Jericho. Imposing. Strong. It consumes your thoughts and saps your strength. It wakes you up and keeps you awake. It is ancient, thick walled, and impenetrable. It is the biggest challenge of your life.

It sits between you and a Promised Land life.

Like Joshua, you can see it.

Like Joshua, you must face it.

And, like Joshua, you don't have to face your Jericho alone.

Now when Joshua was near Jericho, he looked up and saw a man standing in front of him with a drawn sword in his hand. Joshua went up to him and asked, "Are you for us or for our enemies?"

"Neither," he replied, "but as commander of the army of the LORD I have now come." Then Joshua fell facedown to the ground in reverence, and asked him, "What message does my Lord have for his servant?"

The commander of the LORD's army replied, "Take off your sandals, for the place where you are standing is holy." And Joshua did so. (vv. 13–15 NIV)

When it comes to heaven-to-earth communiqués, God seems to follow one rule: there is no rule. In the case of Abram three strangers came for dinner. (Angel food cake for dessert perhaps?) In the story of Moses a blazing bush left him wide eyed and barefoot. A talking donkey got the attention of Balaam. A blazing angel guarded the empty tomb of Jesus.

The Bible is famous for surprise encounters. Yet no visit is more mysterious than this one: the man with the upraised sword and confident air.

Who was he? Let's eliminate some options.

He wasn't an apparition. Nothing in the language leads us to conclude that the person was anything other than flesh and bone. He had muscles that held the sword, vocal cords that created a voice. He wasn't a vision, spirit, ghost, or figment of Joshua's imagination.

Nor was he an angel. We're tempted to think so. After all, angels have swords. Angels can take fleshly form. Angels have courage and defy enemies. But here is the difference: angels do not accept worship. When the apostle John attempted to worship an angel, he was rebuked: "See that you do not do that! I am your fellow servant, and of your brethren who have the testimony of Jesus. Worship God!" (Rev. 19:10). Had this person been an angel, he would have refused Joshua's worship, but this visitor accepted and encouraged it.

Was the guest a human being? A strong, imposing figure? If he was, then he sure had Joshua hoodwinked, for Joshua not only fell at the person's feet out of respect but also removed his sandals.

This guest was no mortal. He wasn't an angel or apparition. That leaves only one option. This was God incarnate. This was Jesus Christ. What Jesus did in Bethlehem for us, he did near Jericho for Joshua. He became flesh and paid his servant a visit. The Commander spoke to his commander.

Do you find this a curious thought? Jesus, BC? Is it difficult to imagine Jesus as an active being before his birth on earth? If so, let me challenge you to widen your imagination. Remember, "Jesus Christ is the same yesterday, today, and forever" (Heb. 13:8). "He was chosen before the creation of the world" (1 Peter 1:20 NIV). The normal restrictions of time and place do not apply to him. We would be wrong to limit his corporal ministry to thirty-three years in Palestine. Long before Jesus ate with Zacchaeus in Jericho, he shared a moment with Joshua near Jericho.

And what a moment it was. "I am the commander of the army of the Lord," Jesus declared. The human eye saw two armies: the Canaanites and the Israelites. Actually, there was a third. The Lord's army, God's angels. This is the heavenly host referred to in Psalm 103:20–21: "Bless the Lord, you mighty angels of his who carry out his orders, listening for each of his commands. Yes, bless the Lord, you armies of his angels who serve him constantly" (TLB).

Dismiss the notion of angels with chiffon wings and rosy cheeks. God's angels were strong enough to close the mouths of lions for Daniel. According to the book of Revelation, it will take only one angel to bind Satan and cast him into a bottomless pit. Just one angel can dispense with the devil.

Imagine what thousands of angels can do! This many exist. Hebrews 12:22 refers to "thousands of angels in joyful assembly" (NIV). When John was given a glimpse into the heavens, he saw too many angels to count: "The number of them was ten thousand times ten thousand, and thousands of thousands" (Rev. 5:11). When God opened the eyes of Elisha's servant, the young man saw that "the mountain was full of horses and chariots of fire all around Elisha" (2 Kings 6:17).

Angels are "ministering spirits sent forth to minister for those who will inherit salvation" (Heb. 1:14). Their presence is a Promised Land perk. All God's children can be sure of God's angels. They are mighty in power. They are many in number. And Jesus is the Commander of them all.

The message to Joshua is unmistakable. *Jericho may have its walls, but, Joshua, you have more. You have God. He is with you.*

Isn't that the word Joshua needed? A reminder of God's mighty presence? Isn't that all any of us need? We need to know that God is near! We are never alone. In our darkest hour, in our deepest questions, the Lord of hosts never leaves us.

When my daughters were small, they would occasionally cry out in the middle of the night. The wind would brush a branch against a window. They would hear a noise on the street. They would shout, "Daddy!"

I would do what all daddies do—tell their mother. Just kidding. I would walk down the hall and step into their room. When I did, the atmosphere changed. Strange noises? Odd sounds? Didn't matter. Daddy was here.

You need to know this: your Father is here. Here as the Commander. Here with his heavenly hosts.

You will never face a Jericho alone.

This is the promise God gave Joy in New Mexico and Joshua near Jericho, and this is the promise he gives to you. He is with you. He is still the Commander of the hosts. "He is in charge of it all, has the final word on everything" (Eph. 1:22 MSG). "He sustains everything by the mighty power of his command" (Heb. 1:3 NLT).

All authority has been given to him. He needs only to lift a finger, and thousands upon thousands of mighty angels will respond to his call.

His presence is a part of your inheritance. "O LORD, You are the portion of my inheritance and my cup" (Ps. 16:5). He will come to you. In the form of a hospital companion or Holy Commander? Perhaps. Or he may come through the word of a scripture or the kindness of a friend. Why, he may even speak to you through a book like this one.

But this much is certain: God comes to his people. "The Commander of the armies of heaven is here among us" (Ps. 46:7 TLB). You are no exception to this promise. His love includes all people. Isn't this the point of the curious dialogue between Joshua and Jesus?

"Are you for us or for our enemies?" Joshua asked.

"Neither," the Commander replied.

God doesn't take sides. He is never against his children. Even the evil Canaanites, who had long ago turned to worshiping idols, were candidates for his mercy. Had Jericho turned and repented, God would have received them as he received Rahab. He is for his children.

And he is for you. "If God is for us, who can be against us?" (Rom. 8:31 NIV).

Are you facing a Jericho-level challenge? Do you face walls that are too high to breach and too thick to crack? Do you face a diagnosis, difficulty, or defeat that keeps you from entering your Promised Land? If so, do what Joshua did.

"When Joshua was by Jericho, . . . *he lifted his eyes* and looked, and behold, a Man stood opposite him" (Josh. 5:13, emphasis mine). After Joshua lifted his eyes, he saw Jesus. As long as our eyes are only on our Jericho, we won't see Jesus. We must look up. "I will lift up my eyes to the hills—From whence comes my help? My help comes from the LORD, Who made heaven and earth" (Ps. 121:1–2).

In late January 1956 Dr. Martin Luther King Jr. received a threatening phone call at his house. It was not the first foreboding message he'd received. But on this night as his children and wife lay sleeping, the weight of the civil rights movement was too heavy. He decided that the risk was too great. He began to map out an exit strategy. At midnight he bowed over the kitchen table and began to pray, "I am afraid. The people are looking to me for leadership, and if I stand before them without strength and courage, they too will falter. I am at the end of my powers. I have nothing left. I've come to the point where I can't face it alone." King described what happened next. "I experienced the presence of the Divine as I had never experienced Him before. It seemed as though I could hear the quiet assurance of an inner voice saying: 'Stand up for righteousness, stand up for truth; and God will be at your side forever.'"[4] When facing a daunting challenge, King shifted his focus and turned to God.

So did Paul and Silas. This missionary duo was thrown into a Roman jail in Philippi. The jailer locked them in the innermost prison. He fastened their feet in stocks. They had no recourse, no means of escape. But rather than look at their shackles and chains, they looked to God. "But at midnight Paul and Silas were praying and singing hymns to God, and the prisoners were listening to them" (Acts 16:25).

It was midnight. They were in the deepest hole of the jail. The doors were locked. The guards were on duty. Yet Paul and Silas were singing and praying. Like Joshua, they looked to God for help.

And, like Joshua, they received it dramatically. "Suddenly there was a great earthquake, so that the foundations of the prison were shaken; and immediately all the doors were opened and everyone's chains were loosed" (v. 26).

Help came after they lifted their eyes.

My friend Tammy Trent made the same discovery. She went to Jamaica with her husband, Trent Lenderink, shortly after their eleventh wedding anniversary. They enjoyed some wonderful island time, and, as they were leaving the area, Trent decided to stop off and check out the blue lagoon, a favorite diving spot on the island. He suited up: wet suit, mask, fins, underwater scooter. Trent's plan was to swim in the blue lagoon for about fifteen minutes. Tammy waited at the water's edge, eating lunch, watching Trent resurface for breath every few minutes. Then she realized she hadn't seen him for a while. Tammy says, "I began to fight back fear when he didn't appear after thirty minutes and then forty-five minutes."

A dive team went to look for Trent. The search continued until night fell, resuming again the next morning, September 11, 2001. Tammy watched the news as the second plane plowed into the twin towers in New York City. Moments later, a call from the dock confirmed that Trent had been found. He had drowned in the lagoon.

Tammy was in shock. The two had been sweethearts since high school. Now she was all alone in a foreign country. She called her parents. All flights were grounded. Tammy's parents could not go to her. She could not leave Jamaica. A couple of days later, Tammy made her way to Kingston, where she and Trent had planned to begin a mission trip. There, alone in a hotel room, Tammy came undone. *God,* she prayed, *if you are up there anywhere, please send somebody to help me, somebody to hold me and let me know that you care and that you see me.*

A few minutes later there was a knock at her hotel door. It was the housekeeper. She was an older Jamaican woman. "I don't mean to bother you," she said, "but I couldn't help but hear you crying, and I was trying to get to you. Could I just come in and hold you and pray for you?"

Tammy broke down in tears. She told the woman what had happened. That kind Jamaican put her arms around Tammy and held her close.

Jesus used a Jamaican housekeeper to comfort his American daughter.[5]

Look to Jesus to comfort you. Turn your gaze away from Jericho. You've looked at it long enough. No need to memorize its circumference or itemize its stones. Healing happens as we look to our Commander. Lift up your eyes and bow your knees. "Joshua fell on his face to the earth and worshiped" (Josh. 5:14).

He was a five-star general. Forty thousand soldiers saluted as he passed. His tent was the Oval Office. Two million people looked up to him. Yet in the presence of God, he fell on his face, removed his sandals, and worshiped.

We are never so strong or mighty that we do not need to worship. Worship-less people have no power greater than themselves to call on. The worship-less heart faces Jericho all alone.

Don't go to your Jericho without first going to your Commander. Let him remind you of the ever-present angels. Let him assure you of his all-encompassing power. He has given you this promise: "I will never fail you. I will never abandon you" (Heb. 13:5 NLT).

Jericho may be strong. But Jesus is stronger. Let him be your strength.

8

WALK CIRCLES AROUND JERICHO

Joshua 6

Here is what you need to know about the walls of Jericho. They were immense. They wrapped around the city like a suit of armor, two concentric circles of stone rising a total of forty feet above the ground. Impenetrable.

Here is what you need to know about Jericho's inhabitants. They were ferocious and barbaric. They withstood all sieges and repelled all invaders. They were guilty of child sacrifice. "They even burn their sons and daughters as sacrifices to their gods!" (Deut. 12:31 NCV). They were a Bronze-age version of the gestapo, ruthless tyrants on the plains of Canaan.[1]

Until the day Joshua showed up. Until the day his army marched in. Until the day the bricks cracked and the boulders broke. Until the day everything shook—the stones of the walls, the knees of the king, the molars of the soldiers. The untoppleable fortress met the unstoppable force.

Mighty Jericho crumbled.

But here is what you need to know about Joshua. He didn't bring the walls down. Joshua's soldiers never swung a hammer. His men never dislodged a brick. They never rammed a door or pried loose a stone. The shaking, quaking, rumbling, and tumbling of the thick, impervious walls? God did that for them.

God will do that for you. Your Jericho is your fear. Your Jericho is your anger, bitterness, or prejudice. Your insecurity about the future. Your guilt about the past. Your negativity, anxiety, and proclivity to criticize, overanalyze, or compartmentalize. Your Jericho is any attitude or mind-set that keeps you from joy, peace, or rest.

Jericho.

It stands between you and your Glory Days. It mocks you and tells you to take your dreams back to the wilderness. It stands like an ogre on the bridge of progress. It is big; it is evil. It blocks your way. And its walls must fall. To live in the Promised Land, you must face your Jericho.

It's not always easy. Every level of inheritance requires a disinheritance from the devil. Satan must be moved off before the saint can move in. Joshua told his people to "go in to possess the land which the LORD your God is giving you to possess" (Josh. 1:11). The verb translated *possess* means "to occupy (by driving out previous tenants, and possessing in their place)."[2]

Satan won't leave without a fight. He will resist. He will push back. But he will not win. Why? Because God has already declared that you are the victor. Satan, defanged and defeated at Calvary, has no authority over you.

God's word to Joshua is God's word to us: "Be strong and of good courage" (v. 6). Do not heed your fear. Do not cower before your woes. Take the land God has given you to possess.

"And the LORD said to Joshua: 'See! I have given Jericho into your hand, its king, and the mighty men of valor'" (6:2).

God did not say, "Joshua, take the city."

God said, "Joshua, receive the city I have taken."

Joshua did not go forth hoping to win. He knew that God had already won.

The same can be said about you and your challenge. God does not say, "Bob, break your bad habit."

He says, "Bob, I have broken the bad habits of your life. Receive the blessing of my victory."

Remember, you are a coheir with Christ. Every attribute of Jesus is at your disposal. Was Jesus victorious? Did he overcome sin and death? Yes! Will you be victorious? Can you overcome sin and death? Yes! The question is not, will you overcome? It is, *when* will you overcome? Life will always bring challenges. But God will always give strength to face them.

Things are different in Canaan. Hang-ups and addictions do not have the last word. Today's problem is not necessarily tomorrow's problem. Don't incarcerate yourself by assuming it is. Resist self-labeling. "I'm just a worrier." "Gossip is my weakness." "My dad was a drinker, and I guess I'll carry on the tradition."

Stop that! These words create alliances with the devil. They grant him access to your spirit. It is not God's will that you live a defeated, marginalized, unhappy, and weary life. Turn a deaf ear to the old voices and make new choices. "The lines have fallen to me in pleasant places; yes, I have a good inheritance" (Ps. 16:6). Live out of your inheritance, not your circumstance.

God has already promised a victory. And he has provided weapons for the fight.

I can picture the soldiers perking up as Joshua, their commander, announces, "It is time to take Jericho!"

"Great!" they reply. "We have our ladders and ropes!"

"We will scale the walls!"

"Our spears are sharpened, and our swords are polished!"

"Which side do we attack first?"

Joshua looks at his men and says, "Well, God has a different strategy." The general outlines the most unlikely of attacks. "Take up the ark of the covenant, and let seven priests bear seven trumpets of rams' horns before the ark of the LORD" (Josh. 6:6).

Joshua commands soldiers to march before and behind the priests. He tells the priests to blow the trumpets continually as they walk around the city once a day. As for the rest of the people? "You shall not shout or make any noise with your voice, nor shall a word proceed out of your mouth, until the day I say to you, 'Shout!' Then you shall shout" (v. 10).

Wait a minute. No war cry? No hand-to-hand combat? No flashing swords, flying spears, battering rams, or catapults? Just priests, rams' horns, marching, and silence? Joshua has at least forty thousand soldiers at his command, and he tells them to be quiet and watch?

What kind of warfare is this?

Spiritual warfare. Every battle, ultimately, is a spiritual battle. Every conflict is a contest with Satan and his forces. Paul urged us to stand "against the wiles of the devil" (Eph. 6:11). The Greek word he used for "wiles" is *methodia*, from which we get our English word *method*.[3] Satan is not passive or fair. He is active and deceptive. He has designs and strategies. Consequently, we need a strategy as well. For that reason "though we walk in the flesh, we do not war according to the flesh. For the weapons of our warfare are not carnal but mighty in God for pulling down strongholds" (2 Cor. 10:3–4).

Just as Jericho was a stronghold in Canaan, we have strongholds in our lives. The apostle Paul used the term to describe a mind-set or attitude. "The weapons of our warfare are . . . mighty in God for pulling down *strongholds*, casting down arguments and every high thing that exalts itself against the knowledge of God" (vv. 4–5, emphasis mine). The apostle defined a stronghold as an argument or high thing that "exalts itself against the knowledge of God." It is a conviction, outlook, or belief that attempts to interfere with truth.

Other translations describe a stronghold as

"imaginations" (KJV),
"pretension" (NIV),
"lofty opinion" (ESV),
"warped philosophies" (MSG).

A stronghold is a false premise that denies God's promise. It "sets itself up against the knowledge of God" (v. 5 NIV). It seeks to eclipse our discovery of God. It attempts to magnify the problem and minimize God's ability to solve it.

Does a stronghold have a strong hold on you? Do you see nothing but Jericho? Do you feel nothing but despair? Do you think thoughts of defeat? Do you speak the language of impossibility?

God could never forgive me. (the stronghold of guilt)

I could never forgive that person. (the stronghold of resentment)

Bad things always happen to me. (the stronghold of self-pity)

I have to be in charge. (the stronghold of pride)

I don't deserve to be loved. (the stronghold of rejection)

I'll never recover. (the stronghold of defeat)

I must be good, or God will reject me. (the stronghold of performance)

I'm only as good as I look. (the stronghold of appearance)

My value equals my possessions. (the stronghold of materialism)

Most Christians don't recognize strongholds.[4] They live in the shadow of these joy-sucking Jerichos.

But we don't have to be among them. Our weapons are from God and have "divine power to demolish strongholds" (v. 4 NIV).

Isn't that what we want? We long to see our strongholds demolished, turned into rubble once and for all, forever and ever, *ka-boom!*

We long to see Jericho brought to the ground. How does this happen?

By keeping God in the center.

The ark of the covenant was the symbol of the Lord's presence. Joshua placed the ark in the middle of the procession. Every activity orbited around God. We don't attack our Jericho with anger, blame casting, or finger-pointing. No, we keep God center stage, using the weapons of worship, Scripture, and prayer. We employ every tool God offers: hymns, songs, communion, Scripture memorization, and petition. We turn off the TV and open the Bible more. We remember Jesus' promise: "I am with you always" (Matt. 28:20). We worry less, pray always. We even blast our version of a ram's horn.

Ram's horn?

The Hebrews used two instruments: the silver trumpet and the ram's horn. The silver trumpet was used to call the people to assemble (Num. 10:2). The ram's horn celebrated a battle already won. When Abraham displayed his willingness to give up his son Isaac as an offering, God stopped him and provided a ram. The ram's horn reminds us of God's sovereign generosity. God gave Abraham a ram of deliverance. God told Joshua to fill the air with sounds of ram's horn victory.

And, curiously, he told the people to keep quiet. "Don't say a word" (Josh. 6:10 NCV). No chitchat. No opinion giving or second-guessing. No whining or chatting. Keep your mouth shut and the trumpets loud.

Imagine the reaction of the Canaanites as Joshua's army marched circles around them. The first day they mocked the Hebrews. The second day they scoffed again but not as loudly. By the fourth and fifth days, the enemy had grown silent. *What are these Hebrews up to?* they wondered. On the sixth day the Canaanites were dry mouthed and wide eyed as the Hebrews made their round. The people of Jericho had never fought a battle like this.

Just as challenging is your battle with your archenemy, the devil. He has held this stronghold in your life for years. You've tried everything to overcome it: renewed discipline, self-help books, pop culture gurus. Nothing helps. But now you come in God's power with God center stage, Jesus in your heart, angels in front and back. You come, not with hope of a possible victory, but with assurance of complete victory.

March like a Promised Land conqueror. Blast your ram's horn. Sing songs of redemption, and declare scriptures of triumph. Marinate your mind with the declaration of Jesus, "It is finished!" (John 19:30), and the announcement of the angels, "He is not here; for He is risen" (Matt. 28:6). Personalize the proclamations of Paul: "We are more than conquerors through [Christ]" (Rom. 8:37), and "I can do all things through Christ" (Phil. 4:13). As you do, the demons will begin to scatter. They have no choice but to leave.

Sometime back a mother asked me to pray for her eight-year-old son. He was troubled by a constant barrage of images and scary visions. He saw people behind cars and in shadows. The images left him withdrawn and timid. They even took his sleep at night.

On the day we met he appeared defeated. His smile was gone. While his other siblings were confident and happy, there was no joy in his face. His eyes often filled with tears, and he clung to his mother.

She had taken him to doctors, but nothing had helped. Would I be willing to pray for him?

I told the young boy what I've been telling you. That the devil has no authority over his life. That the real battles are fought in the mind. That God will help us take every thought captive.

I told him about the spiritual weapons of worship, Scripture, and prayer and urged him to memorize a Bible verse and quote it each time the fearful thoughts came to mind. I gave him a tool. "Reach up with your hand," I urged, "and grab the thought and throw it in the trash. And as quickly as you do that, replace it with a verse of Scripture." We then anointed him with oil and prayed.

Five days later his mother reported great progress. "Since last week the images are gone; he is no longer seeing them. He is doing well in school, and he is enjoying reading the book of Genesis. God gave us Psalm 25:5, 'Lead me in Your truth and teach me, for You are the God of my salvation; on You I wait all the day.' He recites this verse nightly. I believe this has brought him closer to Christ. He uses the strategy of throwing the fearful thoughts away in the trash can. He said when he tried to throw them away, his head would hurt. I asked, 'What made them go away?' He smiled and said, 'I know God made them go away.'"[5]

Another Jericho bites the dust.

"Yell a loud *no* to the Devil and watch him scamper" (James 4:7 MSG). He will retreat. He *must* retreat. He is not allowed in the place where God is praised. Just keep praising and walking.

"But, Max, I've been walking a long time," you say.

Yes, it seems like it. It must have seemed that way to the Hebrews too. Joshua did not tell them how many trips they would have to make around the city. God told Joshua that the walls would fall on the seventh day, but Joshua didn't tell the people. They just kept walking.

Our Joshua didn't tell us either. Through the pen of Paul, Jesus urges us to "be steadfast, immovable, always abounding in the work of the Lord, knowing that your labor is not in vain in the Lord" (1 Cor. 15:58).

Keep walking. For all you know this may be the day the walls come down. You may be only steps from a moment like this.

> On the seventh day . . . they rose early, about the dawning of the day, and marched around the city seven times in the same manner . . . And

the seventh time it happened, when the priests blew the trumpets, that Joshua said to the people: "Shout, for the LORD has given you the city! . . ."

So the people shouted when the priests blew the trumpets. And it happened when the people heard the sound of the trumpet, and the people shouted with a great shout, that the wall fell down flat. Then the people . . . took the city. (Josh. 6:15–16, 20)

The very walls that kept them out became stepping-stones onto which they could climb.

By the way, a great shaking is coming for this world too. Our Joshua, Jesus, will give the signal, and a trumpet will blast. He will reclaim every spoil and repel, once and for all, each demon. He will do again what he did in Canaan.

Until he does, keep marching and believing. Defeat your strongholds with the spiritual weapons of worship, Scripture, and prayer. Move from false premises to God's promises.

It's just a matter of time before your Jericho comes down.

9

DON'T TRUST STUFF

Joshua 7

In our house the game was called "Ladies and Gentlemen." Participants included three preschool-age daughters and one very-happy-to-ham-it-up father. The daughters were freshly bathed, pajama clad, and ready to fly from couch to recliner. The father was glad to serve as the chief ringmaster, spotter, and catapult.

"Ladies and gentlemen," I would announce to the audience of one—Denalyn, who was wondering why we needed to do acrobatics before bedtime. "Ladies and gentlemen, the Lucado girls will now fly through the air."

The living room became a carnival, and I was the human Tilt-A-Whirl. I held the girls upside down and swung them around as if they were rag dolls. They spread their arms and giggled. I tossed them onto the sofa, flipped them over the ottoman, and caught them as they leaped off the back of the recliner. They loved it. Never once did they question my judgment or strength. Their mom did. A pediatrician would have. But never in the cycle of a thousand flips and flops did my daughters say to me,

"Have you thought this through, Dad?"

"I'm not sure you can catch me."

"Are you sure you know how to do this?"

"Perhaps you should practice with a pillow."

Never once did they think I would drop them. *Dad says he can, then he can. Dad says he will, then he will.* They trusted me completely. After all, I was their father.

Oh that we would trust ours.

Jesus once declared, "The work God wants you to do is this: Believe the One he sent" (John 6:29 NCV). Everything begins with faith. The absence of it results in wilderness years. The presence of it results in Promised Land living. It's really that simple. It was for Joshua. He didn't fly through a living room, but he trusted God to open rivers, collapse strongholds, and pry the devil's fingers off his inheritance.

Joshua trusted God. Most of his people followed his example. But one man refused. Achan.

Never heard of the man? You aren't alone. We gravitate toward happier Bible stories. We love Peter's redemption and Saul's conversion and Samson's restoration. But Achan's corruption? Not the stuff of Sunday school songs. Yet his story survived the final edits of the book of Joshua. God kept it for a reason. It's not a happy story nor a pleasant read. You might brace yourself for a solemn warning.

The prior chapter ended on a high note. "So the LORD was with Joshua" (Josh. 6:27 NCV). Jericho was demolished. No rock or enemy was left standing. The stage was set for the Hebrews to run the table. The citadel was in shambles. The word was out, and the Hebrews were emboldened. Joshua's face was on the evening news. "So the LORD was with Joshua, and his fame spread throughout all the country" (v. 27).

So. Such a great word.

Sadly, the *so* in chapter 6 became a *but* in chapter 7.

But Israel violated the instructions about the things set apart for the LORD. A man named Achan had stolen some of these dedicated things, so the LORD was very angry with the Israelites. (Josh. 7:1 NLT)

Here is the dossier on Achan. He had a wife. He had a family. He had oxen, donkeys, sheep, and a tent (v. 24). He had a place in the bloodline of Judah, and, most of all, he blatantly and deliberately violated this command:

Do not take any of the things set apart for destruction, or you yourselves will be completely destroyed, and you will bring trouble on the camp of Israel. Everything made from silver, gold, bronze, or iron is sacred to the LORD and must be brought into his treasury. (6:18–19 NLT)

The instructions were clear. Don't touch the stuff. Don't make necklaces out of the gold. Don't make medals out of the bronze. No souvenirs. No trinkets. No Jericho jewelry.

No kidding.

God had high hopes for these Hebrew people. Through them the Scriptures would be written, the prophets would come, and the Messiah would descend. God needed them to trust him and him alone. Rely on their own strength? No. Their own resources? No. Their own ability? No.

God is enough. Hasn't this been the message of Joshua thus far? Who opened the Jordan River? Who led the people across on dry ground? Who appeared to encourage Joshua? Who brought down the Jericho walls? Who has fought for and delivered the people?

God!

He cared for his people. Even in the wilderness they never went without provision. They may have grown weary of manna-nut bread, but they were never hungry.

He gave them not just food but clothing and good health. Moses once reminded the Hebrews, "Your clothes did not wear out and your feet did not swell during these forty years" (Deut. 8:4 NIV). God echoed the message: "During the forty years that I led you through the wilderness, your clothes did not wear out, nor did the sandals on your feet" (Deut. 29:5 NIV).

The following phrases were never heard in the wilderness:

"I need to soak my feet in Epsom salts."

"Oh, bummer, my robe has another rip in it."

"Hey, new sandals. Where did you get them?"

Podiatrists, tailors, and cobblers had a lot of time on their hands.

No want for food. No need for clothing. Never a blister or a bunion. God provided for them. And God promised to provide more.

Again quoting Moses:

For the LORD your God is bringing you into a good land—a land with brooks, streams, and deep springs gushing out into the valleys and hills; a land with wheat and barley, vines and fig trees, pomegranates, olive oil and honey; a land where bread will not be scarce and you will lack nothing; a land where the rocks are iron and you can dig copper out of the hills. (Deut. 8:7–9 NIV)

In God's Promised Land society he was the sole source of blessings. He knew what would happen if the soldiers collected treasures. They would stop trusting him and start trusting stuff. Think about it. They were simple hayseed bedouin, most of them conceived and born in the wilderness. Hebrews in Jericho were like gypsies on Rodeo Drive. The gold would bedazzle them. The bracelets and rings would entrance them. The shekels, the jewelry, the silk . . . the Hebrews were ill prepared to own such booty.

Achan proved the point. He saw the bling and forgot his King. And God's discipline was immediate and severe.

A few miles north of Jericho sat the encampment of Ai. Joshua circled the name of the city on his wall map and told his officers to attack. Flush with a Jericho victory, he assumed the small town would be easy pickins. The entire village numbered only twelve thousand. Joshua had that many men on his night watch. So he sent a reduced battalion: three thousand soldiers.

Joshua was in for a surprise. The town was a kennel of pit bulls. The people of Ai bit back. Joshua's division raced home discouraged, disheveled, and licking their wounds. In fact, we wonder if the village of Ai got its name from the cry of the Hebrews who ran back to Joshua yelling "Ai-yi-yi-yi!"

> The men of Ai chased the Israelites from the town gate as far as the quarries, and they killed about thirty-six who were retreating down the slope. The Israelites were paralyzed with fear at this turn of events, and their courage melted away. (Josh. 7:4–5 NLT)

Joshua's mighty men crawled beneath their blankets and trembled. He didn't know what to think. He was coming off a string of victories and miracles. Jordan. Jericho. The rescue of Rahab. Undefeated. Undaunted. Undeniably the new force in Canaan—and now this?

Our hero had a meltdown. He tore his clothing and fell on his face. He prayed like the Hebrews of the wilderness days. He regretted the invasion and accused God of setting them up for certain defeat. "Oh, that we had been content, and dwelt on the other side of the Jordan!" (v. 7).

Joshua came undone, but God was not done. "[T]he LORD said to Joshua, 'Get up! Why are you lying on your face like this?'" (v. 10 NLT).

Joshua pulled himself to his feet. God told him that there was trouble in the camp.

> Israel has sinned and broken my covenant! They have stolen some of the things that I commanded must be set apart for me. And they have not only stolen them but have lied about it and hidden the things among their own belongings. That is why the Israelites are running from their enemies in defeat. (vv. 11–12 NLT)

It's not that the people of Ai were formidable. It's more that the Hebrew camp was poisoned. God told Joshua, in so many words, to find the rotten apple before it ruined the whole bushel.

At God's direction Joshua did a tribe-by-tribe, then family-by-family, then man-by-man review until Achan confessed. The treasures were hidden in his tent.

> I have sinned against the LORD, the God of Israel. Among the plunder I saw a beautiful robe from Babylon, 200 silver coins, and a bar of gold weighing more than a pound. I wanted them so much that I took them. They are hidden in the ground beneath my tent, with the silver buried deeper than the rest. (vv. 20–21 NLT)

It's not hard to re-create Achan's stumble. Along with other soldiers he had walked through the fallen city. Walls down. Rubble everywhere. Conquest complete. All the spoils of Jericho lay unprotected—the gold, coins, fine garments. Everyone saw the stuff. Everyone else remembered God's command. They saw the treasures and kept going.

But Achan? When he thought no one was looking, he paused, cast a glimpse to the right and a glimpse to the left. "I *saw* a beautiful robe from Babylon, 200 silver coins, and a bar of gold weighing more than a pound. I *wanted* them so much that I *took* them."

"I saw . . . I wanted . . . I took."

Others saw. Others surely wanted. But only Achan took. Why?

Perhaps he wanted a payoff. After all, his side had won the battle. Or an ace in the hole, some money to fall back on in case the Hebrews lost. A nest egg would be nice, as would some negotiating power in case he was taken captive.

Whatever the explanation, Achan didn't trust God. He didn't trust God's wisdom. He didn't trust God's ability to provide or protect. In the biblical version of "Ladies and Gentlemen," Achan doubted God's ability to catch him. So he broke the preinvasion oath he and the others had made. This was the indictment God gave: "he has transgressed the covenant of the LORD" (Josh. 7:15). Achan must have been among the men who pledged, "Whoever rebels against your [Joshua's] word and does not obey it, whatever you may command them, will be put to death" (1:18 NIV). Achan took matters into his own hands. More literally, he took treasure into his tent and entangled his family in his deceit.

The judgment was swift and punishment stiff. Achan and his family were publicly executed, their possessions burned. A monument was built as a warning to the people. It was a solemn day in Gilgal.

This is a solemn warning to us. God is jealous for our trust. He doesn't request it, suggest it, or recommend it; he demands it. His unvarnished message is clear: "Trust me and me alone."

A similar unraveling happened in the New Testament. The church had begun its own era of Glory Days. Miracles, sermons, baptisms, and growth. The book of Acts is all good fruit and fanfare, until chapter 5. Until Ananias and Sapphira. Like Achan, this couple stole what belonged to God. They pledged to sell some property and give the money to the church. When they changed their minds about the gift, they acted as if they hadn't.

Like Achan, they lied. Like Achan, they died. Their bodies were carried out, and "great fear gripped the entire church" (Acts 5:11 NLT). On this topic of faith God is serious. Dead serious.

Achan in Gilgal.

Ananias and Sapphira in Jerusalem.

Their graves remind us: be careful.

What would a search of your tent reveal?

A cabinet full of faith or a closet piled with ambition? A pantry of hope or a storage bin of stock certificates?

For our own sakes the story of Achan reminds us, don't put your trust in stuff.

Paul told Timothy, "Command those who are rich in this present world not to be arrogant nor to put their hope in wealth, which is so uncertain, but to put their hope in God, who richly provides us with everything for our enjoyment" (1 Tim. 6:17 NIV).

The "rich in this . . . world." That is you. That is me. If you have enough education to read this page, enough resources to own this book, you likely qualify as a prosperous person. And that is okay. Prosperity is a common consequence of faithfulness (Prov. 22:4). Paul didn't tell the rich to feel guilty about being rich; he just urged caution.

Nothing breeds failure like success.

Money is just a short-term condition. The abundance or lack of money will only be felt for one life . . . so don't get tangled up in it.

Imagine you were living in the South during the Civil War and had accumulated large amounts of Confederate currency. Through a series of events you became convinced that the South was going to lose and your money would soon be worthless. What would you do? If you had any common sense, you would get rid of your Southern cents. You'd put every penny you could into the currency that is to come and prepare yourself for the end of the war.

Are you investing in the currency of heaven? The world economy is going down. Your wallet is full of soon-to-be-useless paper. The currency of this world will be worth nothing when you die or when Christ returns, both of which could happen at any moment. If you and I stockpile earthly treasures and not heavenly treasures, what does that say about where we put our trust?

Glory Days happen to the degree that we trust him.

Whom do you trust? God or King More? King More is a rotten ruler. He never satisfies. He rusts. He rots. He loses his value. He goes out of style. For all the promises he makes, he cannot keep a single one. King More will break your heart.

But the King of kings? He will catch you every single time.

10

NO FAILURE
IS FATAL

Joshua 8:1–29

I have a distinct memory from the 1991 Super Bowl. I'm not a football junkie. Nor do I have extraordinary recall. Truth is, I don't remember anything about the '91 football season except this one detail. A headline. An observation prompted by Scott Norwood's kick.

He played for the Buffalo Bills. The city of Buffalo hadn't won a major sports championship since 1965. But that night in Tampa Bay it appeared the ball would finally bounce the Bills' way. They went back and forth with the New York Giants. With seconds to go they were a point down. They reached the Giants' twenty-nine yard line. There was time for only one more play. They turned to their kicker, Scott Norwood. All-Pro. Leading scorer of the team. As predictable as snow in Buffalo. One season he made thirty-two of thirty-seven attempts. He'd scored from this distance five times during the season. He needed to do it a sixth time.

The world watched as Norwood went through his prekick routine. He tuned out the crowd, selected a target line, got a feel for the timing, waited for the snap, and kicked the ball. He kept his head down and followed through. By the time he looked up, the ball was three quarters of the way to the goal. That's when he realized he'd missed.

The wrong sideline erupted.

All of Buffalo groaned.

Norwood hung his head.

The headline would read "Wide and to the right: The kick that will forever haunt Scott Norwood."[1]

No do-overs. No second chance. No reprieve. He couldn't rewind the tape and create a different result. He had to live with the consequences.

So did Joshua. He had suffered a humiliating loss. The people of Ai, though fewer in number, had proved greater in might. They had pounced on Joshua's men, resulting in an unexpected defeat. One of the soldiers, it was learned, had disobeyed God's earlier command. The commander was left with the distasteful, unpleasant task of exposing and punishing the rebellion.

Joshua offered a prayer right out of *The Wilderness Book of Common Complaint*: "Alas, Lord GOD, why have You brought this people over the Jordan at all—to deliver us into the hand of the Amorites, to destroy us?" (Josh. 7:7).

Not one of his better days.

The guy had been making field goals his entire life. He showed courage as a spy for Moses. He assumed the mantle of leadership. He didn't hesitate at the Jordan. He didn't flinch at Jericho. But in the episode called "Achan's Deceit and Ai's Defeat"? He failed. In front of his army, in front of the enemy, in front of God . . . he failed.

Joshua dragged himself back to his tent. The entire camp was somber. They had buried thirty-six of their soldiers and witnessed the downfall of a countryman.

Joshua sensed the glares and stares of the people.

Joshua's not a good leader.

He doesn't have what it takes.

He's let us down.

He knew what they thought. Worse still, he knew what he thought. His mind sloshed with self-doubt.

What was I thinking when I took this job?

I should've done better.

It's all my fault.

The voices—he heard them all.

So did you.

When you lost your job, flunked the exam, dropped out of school. When your marriage went south. When your business went broke. When you failed. The voices began to howl. Monkeys in a cage, they were, laughing at you. You heard them.

And you joined them! You disqualified yourself, berated yourself, upbraided yourself. You sentenced yourself to a life of hard labor in the Leavenworth of poor self-worth.

Oh, the voices of failure.

Failure finds us all. Failure is so universal we have to wonder why more self-help gurus don't address it. Bookstores overflow with volumes on how to succeed. But you'll look a long time before you find a section called "How to Succeed at Failing."

Maybe no one knows what to say. But God does. His book is written for failures. It is full of folks who were foul-ups and flops. David was a moral failure, yet God used him. Elijah was an emotional train wreck after Mount Carmel, but God blessed him. Jonah was in the belly of a fish when he prayed his most honest prayer, and God heard it.

Perfect people? No. Perfect messes? You bet. Yet God used them. A surprising and welcome discovery of the Bible is this: God uses failures.

God used Joshua's failure to show us what to do with ours. God quickly and urgently called Joshua to get on with life.

"Get up! Why do you lie thus on your face?" (7:10).

"Do not be afraid, nor be dismayed; take all the people of war with you, and arise, go up to Ai" (8:1).

Failure is a form of quicksand. Take immediate action or you'll be sucked under.

One stumble does not define or break a person. Though you failed, God's love does not. Face your failures with faith in God's goodness. He saw this collapse coming. When you stood on the eastern side of the Jordan, God could see the upcoming mishap of your Ai.

Still, he tells you what he told Joshua: "Arise, go . . . , you and all this people, to the land which I am giving" (1:2). There is no condition in that covenant. No fine print. No performance language. God's Promised Land offer does not depend on your perfection. It depends on his.

In God's hands no defeat is a crushing defeat. "The steps of good men are directed by the Lord. He delights in each step they take. If they fall, it isn't fatal, for the Lord holds them with his hand" (Ps. 37:23–24 TLB).

How essential it is that you understand this. Miss this truth and miss your Glory Days. You must believe that God's grace is greater than your failures. Pitch your tent on promises like this one: "There is now no condemnation for those who are in Christ Jesus . . . who do not walk according to the flesh but according to the Spirit" (Rom. 8:1, 4 NASB).

Everyone stumbles. The difference is in the response. Some stumble into the pit of guilt. Others tumble into the arms of God. Those who find grace do so because they "walk according . . . to the Spirit." They hear God's voice. They make a deliberate decision to stand up and lean into God's grace.

As God told Joshua, "Do not be afraid, nor . . . dismayed; . . . *arise, go . . .*"

The prodigal son did this. He resolved, "I will arise and go to my father" (Luke 15:18).

Remember his story? Just like you, he was given an inheritance; he was a member of the family. Perhaps just like you, he squandered it on wild living and bad choices. He lost every penny. His trail dead-ended in a pigpen. He fed hogs for a living.

One day he was so hungry that the slop smelled like sirloin. He leaned over the trough, took a sniff, and drooled. He tied a napkin around his neck and pulled a fork out of his pocket and sprinkled salt on the slop. He was just about to dig in when something within him awoke. *Wait a second. What am I doing wallowing in the mud, rubbing shoulders with the swine?* Then he made a decision that changed his life forever. "I will arise and go to my father."

You can do that! Perhaps you can't solve all your problems or disentangle all your knots. You can't undo all the damage you've done. But you can arise and go to your Father.

Landing in a pigpen stinks. But staying there is just plain stupid.

Rise up and step out. Even the apostle Paul had to make this choice. "I leave the past behind and with hands outstretched to whatever lies ahead I go straight for the goal" (Phil. 3:13–14 PHILLIPS).

There ain't no future in the past. You can't change yesterday, but you can do something about tomorrow. *Put God's plan in place.*

God told Joshua to revisit the place of failure. "Arise, go up to Ai. See, I have given into your hand the king of Ai, his people, his city, and his land" (Josh. 8:1). In essence God told Joshua, "Let's do it again. This time my way."

Joshua didn't need to be told twice. He and his men made an early morning march from Gilgal to Ai, a distance of about fifteen miles. He positioned a crack commando unit behind the town.[2] Behind this contingent was a corps of five thousand men (v. 12).

Joshua then took another company of soldiers. They headed in the direction of the city. The plan was straight out of basic military tactics. Joshua would attack, then retreat, luring the soldiers of Ai away from their village. It worked.

The king of Ai, still strutting from victory number one, set out for victory number two. He marched toward Joshua, leaving the town unprotected. The elite squad charged in and set fire to the city. And Joshua reversed his course, catching the army of Ai in the middle. The victory was complete.

Contrast this attack with the first one. In the first, Joshua consulted spies; in the second, he listened to God. In the first, he stayed home. In the second, he led the way. The first attack involved a small unit. His second involved many more men. The first attack involved no tactics. His second was strategic and sophisticated.

The point? God gave Joshua a new plan: Try again, my way. When he followed God's strategy, victory happened.

Peter, too, discovered the wonder of God's second chance. One day Jesus used his boat as a platform. The crowd on the beach was so great that Jesus needed a buffer. So he preached from Peter's boat. Then he told Peter to take him fishing.

The apostle-to-be had no interest. He was tired; he had fished all night. He was discouraged; he had caught nothing. He was dubious. What did Jesus know about catching fish? Peter was self-conscious. People packed the beach. Who wants to fail in public?

But Jesus insisted. And Peter relented. "At Your word I will let down the net" (Luke 5:5).

This was a moment of truth for Peter. He was saying, "I will try again, your way." When he did, the catch of fish was so great the boat nearly sank. Sometimes we just need to try again with Christ in the boat.

Failures are fatal only if we fail to learn from them.

My wife and I spent five years on a missionary team in Rio de

Janeiro, Brazil. Our first two years felt fruitless and futile. We grin-
gos typically outnumbered the Brazilians in the worship service.
More often than not I went home frustrated.

So we asked God for another plan. We prayed and reread the
Epistles. We especially focused on Galatians. It occurred to me that
I was preaching a limited grace. When I compared our gospel message with Paul's, I saw a difference. His was high-octane good news.
Mine was soured legalism. So as a team we resolved to focus on the
gospel. In my teaching I did my best to proclaim forgiveness of sins
and resurrection from the dead.

We saw an immediate change. We baptized forty people in twelve
months! Quite a few for a church of sixty members. God wasn't finished with us. We just needed to put the past in the past and God's
plan in place.

Don't spend another minute in the pigpen. It's time to rise up.

Don't waste your failures by failing to learn from them. It's time
to wise up.

God has not forgotten you. Keep your head up. You never know
what good awaits you.

Scott Norwood walked off the football field with his head down.
For a couple of days thoughts of the missed kick never left him. He
couldn't sleep. He couldn't find peace. He was still upset when the
team returned to Buffalo. In spite of the loss the city hosted an event
to honor the team. The turnout was huge—between twenty-five and
thirty thousand people. Norwood attended and took his place on the
platform with the other players.

He attempted to linger in the background, hidden behind the
others. But the fans had something else in mind. In the middle of a
civic leader's speech, this chant began:

"We want Scott."

The chant grew louder.

"We want Scott!"

Scott remained behind his teammates. After all, he didn't know why the crowd wanted him.

The chant grew in volume until the speaker had to stop. Norwood's teammates pushed him to the front of the stage. When the fans saw Scott, they gave him a rousing ovation. He missed the kick, but they made sure he knew he was still a part of their community.

The Bible says that we are surrounded by a great cloud of witnesses (Heb. 12:1). Thousands upon thousands of saved saints are looking down on us. Abraham. Peter. David. Paul . . . and Joshua. Your grandma, uncle, neighbor, coach. They've seen God's great grace, and they are all pulling for you.

Press your ear against the curtain of eternity and listen. Do you hear them? They are chanting your name. They are pulling for you to keep going.

"Don't quit!"

"It's worth it!"

"Try again!"

You may have missed a goal, but you're still a part of God's team.

11

VOICES, CHOICES, AND CONSEQUENCES

Joshua 8:30–35

The last words I remember hearing before I descended into the water were "You're gonna regret it." I waved away the warning without turning around. What was to regret? Everyone else was taking the long way; I took the shortcut. Let the others walk around the water; I would wade through it. After all, it was just the Everglades.

Of course, I had never been in the Everglades before. I'd never seen a Florida swamp. I'd seen creeks in Texas, lakes in New Mexico. Why, I'd even been trout fishing in a Colorado river. Water is water, right?

"Wrong," my newfound Florida friends tried to tell me. They were taking me to a picnic. A welcome-to-Miami party. The tables sat on the other side of a marsh. The parks department had kindly constructed a bridge by which pedestrians could pass over the marsh. But who needed a bridge? I was fresh out of college, single, eager to impress, and undaunted at the sight of a few yards of water.

"I'll wade across."

Someone pointed at the sign. "Swamp water not recommended for recreation."

I couldn't be slowed by a warning, so I ventured in. The mud swallowed my feet. The brine was murky, smelly, and home to a million mosquitoes. Squiggly things swam past me. Scaly things brushed against me. I think I saw a set of eyeballs peering in my direction.

I backpedaled. Both flip-flops were sucked into the abyss, never to be seen again. I exited, mud covered, mosquito bitten, and red faced. I walked over the bridge and took my seat at the picnic table.

Everyone else enjoyed the picnic. I pretended to, but how could I? Sitting there covered in dried mud, mosquito welts, and regrets.

Made for a miserable picnic.

Makes for an apt proverb.

Life comes with voices. Voices lead to choices. Choices have consequences.

Why do some Christians grumble at the picnic? Why do some saints thrive while others scramble to survive? Why do some tackle Everest-size challenges and succeed while others walk seemingly downhill paths and stumble? Why are some people unquenchably content while others are inexplicably unhappy?

I've wondered this in my own life. Some seasons feel like a downhill, downwind bike ride. Others are like pedaling a flat-tired unicycle up Pikes Peak. Why?

The answer comes back to swamps, signs, and chosen paths.

Glory Days happen when we make good choices. Trouble happens when we don't. This is the headline message delivered by Joshua in the nationwide assembly in the Valley of Shechem.

As you compile your list of key geographical touchstones in the book of Joshua, don't overlook this one. The list includes

- the Jordan River (site of the crossing);
- the Gilgal encampment (the stones of remembrance and renewal of circumcision);

- Jericho (where Joshua saw the Commander and the walls fell);
- Ai (where Achan fell and Joshua rebounded);
- and now Shechem.

The pilgrimage to Shechem was Moses' idea (Deut. 27:4–8). He had instructed Joshua to bring the invasion to a halt and every person to the Valley of Shechem. Shechem was a twenty-mile hike from the Hebrew encampment at Gilgal.[1] The Hebrews must have looked like an Amazon River of humanity as they marched.

Once they reached the valley, Joshua set about the task of building an altar.

> Now Joshua built an altar to the LORD God of Israel in Mount Ebal, as Moses the servant of the LORD had commanded the children of Israel, as it is written in the Book of the Law of Moses: "an altar of whole stones over which no man has wielded an iron tool." And they offered on it burnt offerings to the LORD, and sacrificed peace offerings. And there, in the presence of the children of Israel, he wrote on the stones a copy of the law of Moses, which he had written. (Josh. 8:30–32)

In the ancient Near East it was customary for kings to commemorate their military achievements by recording their conquests on huge stones covered with plaster. Joshua, however, didn't memorialize his work. He celebrated God's law. The secret to the successful campaign of the Hebrews was not the strength of the army but the resolve of the people to keep God's commandments.

And then the best part:

> Then all Israel, with their elders and officers and judges, stood on either side of the ark before the priests, the Levites, who bore the ark

of the covenant of the LORD, the stranger as well as he who was born among them. Half of them were in front of Mount Gerizim and half of them in front of Mount Ebal, as Moses the servant of the LORD had commanded before, that they should bless the people of Israel. And afterward he read all the words of the law, the blessings and the cursings, according to all that is written in the Book of the Law. (vv. 33–34)

The meadows of Shechem sit between Mount Ebal and Mount Gerizim. Gardens, orchards, and olive groves grow throughout the valley. Limestone stratum sits in the deepest part of the crevice, broken into ledges "so as to present the appearance of a series of regular benches."[2] The rock formation creates an amphitheater with acoustic properties that allow a sound originating on one side of the valley to be heard on the other.

The tribes were assigned their places: six on one side and six on the other. Midway between stood the priests, Levites, leaders, and the ark of the covenant. When Joshua and the Levites read the blessings, the tribes standing on Gerizim shouted, "Amen!" When the leaders read the curses, the million or so people on Ebal declared, "Amen!"[3]

Can you imagine the drama of the moment?

"If you listen obediently to the voice of God, he will . . .

"Defeat your enemies!"
"Amen!"
"Order a blessing on your barns!"
"Amen!"
"Lavish you with good things!"
"Amen!"
"Throw open the doors of his sky vaults and pour rain on your land" (see Deut. 28:1–13).
"Amen!"

The proclamation of the curses followed the same pattern. "Cursed is anyone who . . .

"Carves a god image!"
"Amen!"
"Demeans a parent!"
"Amen!"
"Takes a bribe to kill an innocent person."
"Amen!" (see Deut. 27).

Back and forth, back and forth. Voices reverberated off the stone cliffs. All the people—children, immigrants, old-timers, everyone—in antiphonal rhythm proclaimed their values. "There was not a word of all that Moses had commanded which Joshua did not read before all the assembly of Israel, with the women, the little ones, and the strangers who were living among them" (Josh. 8:35).

Keep in mind the when and where of this assembly. When did this event happen? In the midst of an invasion. Where? Smack-dab in the middle of enemy territory. These desert-toughened people pressed the Pause button on the physical battle in order to fight the spiritual one.

Heeding God's Word is more critical than fighting God's war. Indeed, heeding God's Word *is* fighting God's war. Conquest happens as the covenant is honored.

Do you want a Promised Land life?

Desire the fullness of Glory Days?

Want to experience Canaan to the fullest?

Obey God's commands.

What's that? You expected something more mystical, exotic, intriguing? You thought that the Canaan-level life was birthed from ecstatic utterances or angelic visions, mountaintop moments or midnight messages from heaven?

Sorry to disappoint you. "Obedience," wrote C. S. Lewis, "is the key to all doors."⁴ Don't think for a second that you can heed the wrong voice, make the wrong choice, and escape the consequences.

At the same time, obedience leads to a waterfall of goodness not just for you but for your children, children's children, great-grand-children, and the children of a thousand generations in the future. God promises to show "love to a thousand generations of those who love me and keep my commandments" (Ex. 20:6 NIV).

As we obey God's commands, we open the door for God's favor.

Case in point? The remarkable change of Pitcairn Island. In the spring of 1789 a band of mutinous sailors settled on this tiny dot four thousand miles east of New Zealand in the South Pacific. Angered by the harsh rule of Captain Bligh, the mutineers had given him and his followers the boot and a boat and watched them float out to sea.

Captain Bligh made it to safety and eventually testified against the crew of the ship called HMS *Bounty*. But what became of those sailors who settled on Pitcairn? The men took Tahitian wives and recruited Tahitian workers. They had the opportunity to create a stable society, but instead they created a sinkhole of violence, adultery, and drunkenness. They elevated no standard, no morals, no laws. Within a decade they were dead from disease and attacks. Only one mutineer survived. Alexander Smith.

Left on the two-square-mile island, he began to read the Bible. He later testified, "When I came to the Life of Jesus, my heart began to open like doors swingin' apart. Once I was sure God was a loving and merciful Father to them that repent, it seemed to me I could feel His very presence . . . and I grew more sure every day of His guiding hand."

Smith convinced the islanders to follow the teachings of Scripture. When the British navy discovered Pitcairn Island in 1808, they were stunned by the order and decency. The island was transformed.

Smith was pardoned, and Pitcairn became synonymous for piety in the nineteenth century.[5]

Obedience leads to blessing. Disobedience leads to trouble.

Remember Jesus' parable about the two builders who each built a house? One built on cheap, easy-to-access sand. The other built on costly, difficult-to-reach rock. The second construction project demanded more time and expense, but when the spring rains turned the creek into a gulley washer, guess which builder enjoyed a blessing and which experienced trouble? Beachfront property doesn't make for much if it can't withstand the storm.

According to Jesus the wise builder is "whoever hears these sayings of Mine, and does them" (Matt. 7:24). Both builders heard the teachings. The difference between the two was not knowledge and ignorance but obedience and disobedience. Security comes as we put God's precepts into practice. We're only as strong as our obedience. "Be doers of the word, and not hearers only, deceiving yourselves" (James 1:22).

A few months back I was in New York City on a ministry trip. I had spent the day in the company of coworkers and friends. The final engagement of the evening concluded around ten o'clock. As we entered the hotel lobby, my stomach growled. I was hungry. My colleagues weren't. They had eaten during the banquet at which I spoke. I considered going to the room and ordering room service. But the hotel was busy, and the delivery would be late. I remembered a delicatessen nearby, so I told the team good night and headed down the street.

Within a few minutes I was on my way back, sandwich in hand. As I crossed the street, two women were standing on the corner near my hotel. I assumed they had just left the theater.

"Excuse me, sir," one of them said. "Could you use some company tonight?"

I was taken aback. Young women don't flirt with me. I'm sixty years old. My hair is falling out. I fight the battle of the belly bulge. I haven't popped a bicep since Clinton was in office. Then it dawned on me; they weren't interested in me. They were interested in what I might pay them. This verse popped into my thoughts: "Do not be deceived, God is not mocked; for whatever a man sows, that he will also reap" (Gal. 6:7).

I didn't even stop. I waved them off, hurried to my hotel room, and called my wife. Imagine if I hadn't. Imagine the pain, the guilt, the shame I would have created. Talk about a swampland.

Voices await you today. Maybe not on a New York City avenue but at work, in your cul-de-sac, at school, on the Internet. They're waiting for you. They stand on the intersections of your social life and family. You can't eliminate their presence. But you can prepare for their invitation.

Remember who you are; you are God's child. You've been bought by the most precious commodity in the history of the universe: the blood of Christ. You are indwelled by the Spirit of the living God. You are being equipped for an eternal assignment that will empower you to live in the very presence of God. You have been set apart for a holy calling. You are his.

Remember where you are; this is Canaan. You are in the Promised Land, not geographically but spiritually. This is the land of grace and hope and freedom and truth and love and life. The devil has no jurisdiction over you. He acts as if he does. He walks with a swagger and brings temptation, but as you resist him and turn to God, he must flee (James 4:7).

Decide now what you will say then.

Choose obedience. And, as you do, you can expect blessings: the blessing of a clean conscience, the blessing of a good night's sleep, the blessing of God's fellowship, the blessing of God's favor. This is no guarantee of an easy life. It is the assurance of God's help. "The good man does not escape all troubles—he has them too. But the Lord helps him in each and every one" (Ps. 34:19 TLB).

One final thought before we leave the Valley of Shechem. Take note of the altar's location. The altar made with unhewed stone—where was it built? Not on Gerizim, the mount of blessing. Joshua built it on Ebal, the hill of the cursing. Even in the midst of poor choices, there is grace.

May we hear the right voice. May we make the right choice. May we enjoy blessing upon blessing.

But if we don't, may we return to the altar on Ebal. It was built for people like us.

12
___

PRAY AUDACIOUS PRAYERS

Joshua 9–10

When Martin Luther's coworker became ill, the reformer prayed boldly for healing. "I besought the Almighty with great vigor," he wrote. "I attacked him with his own weapons, quoting from Scripture all the promises I could remember, that prayers should be granted, and said that he must grant my prayer, if I was henceforth to put faith in his promises."[1]

On another occasion his good friend Frederick Myconius was sick. Luther wrote to him: "I command thee in the name of God to live because I still have need of thee in the work of reforming the church . . . The Lord will never let me hear that thou art dead, but will permit thee to survive me. For this I am praying, this is my will, and may my will be done, because I seek only to glorify the name of God."[2]

As John Wesley was crossing the Atlantic Ocean, contrary winds came up. He was reading in his cabin when he became aware of some confusion on board. When he learned that the winds were knocking the ship off course, he responded in prayer. Adam Clarke, a colleague, heard the prayer and recorded it.

Almighty and everlasting God, thou hast sway everywhere, and all things serve the purpose of thy will, thou holdest the winds in thy fists and sittest upon the water floods, and reignest a king for ever. Command these winds and these waves that they obey thee, and take us speedily and safely to the haven whither we would go.

Wesley stood up from his knees, took up his book, and continued to read. Dr. Clarke went on deck, where he found calm winds and the ship on course. But Wesley made no remark about the answered prayer. Clarke wrote, "So fully did he expect to be heard that he took it for granted that he was heard."[3]

How bold are your prayers?

Boldness in prayer is an uncomfortable thought for many. We think of speaking softly to God, humbling ourselves before God, or having a chat with God . . . but agonizing before God? Storming heaven with prayers? Pounding on the door of the Most High? Wrestling with God? Isn't such prayer irreverent? Presumptuous?

It would be had God not invited us to pray as such. "So let us come boldly to the very throne of God and stay there to receive his mercy and to find grace to help us in our times of need" (Heb. 4:16 TLB).

Joshua did this, but not before he didn't. His prayer life teaches us what happens when we *don't* pray as much as it tells us *how* to pray.

In the days following the Shechem gathering, a group of strangers entered Joshua's camp. They told him, "From a very far country your servants have come" (Josh. 9:9). They presented themselves as hapless pilgrims from a distant place. Everything seemed to fit their story. Their grain sacks, sandals, and clothes were worn-out. Even their bread was moldy and dry. They claimed to be allies of the Hebrews. They praised the accomplishments of God and asked Joshua and his men to make a covenant with them. Joshua weighed the options, and his rulers eventually agreed.

Three days passed before Joshua realized he had been snook-ered. These people were not from a distant land; they were from Gibeon, only a day's walk away. Their weathered clothing was a dis-guise. They pretended to be foreigners because they knew that the Hebrews had ransacked Jericho and Ai. They may have known that God's laws had made special provision for cities outside of Canaan (Deut. 20:10–12). Any city that agreed to make peace would be spared. So, being afraid, they resorted to deception.

Why didn't Joshua and the elders detect the ruse? "They did not ask counsel of the LORD" (Josh. 9:14). The practice of the Hebrews was supposed to be pray first, act later. Joshua was told to "stand before Eleazar the priest, who shall inquire before the LORD" (Num. 27:21).

Joshua failed to do this. He and his council entered into an alli-ance with the enemy because they didn't seek the counsel of God.

We do well to learn from Joshua's mistake. Our enemy enters our camp in a disguise as well. "Satan himself masquerades as an angel of light" (2 Cor. 11:14 NIV). He is crafty. That's why it is essen-tial that we . . .

Consult God in everything. Always. Immediately. Quickly. Live with one ear toward heaven. Keep the line open to God.

"Is this opportunity from you, God?"

"Are you in this venture, God?"

"Should I take this road, God?"

At every decision. At each crossroads. Acknowledge him, heed him, ask him, "Do I turn right or left?" "Trust in the LORD with all your heart, and lean not on your own understanding; in all your ways acknowledge Him, and He shall direct your paths" (Prov. 3:5–6).

Our relationship with God is exactly that, a relationship. His invitation is clear and simple: "Come and talk with me, O my people" (Ps. 27:8 TLB). And our response? "Lord, I am coming" (v. 8 TLB).

We abide with him, and he abides with us. He grants wisdom as we need it.

I once tried giving Denalyn this level of guidance. We were using the GPS on my smartphone to locate a particular destination. Denalyn was driving, and I was reading the map. Just for the fun of it, I muted the volume on the voice and told Denalyn that I would share the direction at the moment she needed it, not before.

She did not like that plan. She wanted to know the entire itinerary at once. She preferred to have all the information rather than bits and pieces of it.

But I insisted. I told her, "This is good spiritual training. God works this way."

"But you're not God."

Good point. I told her the entire itinerary.

But God doesn't. He will help us against the devil. He will disclose the craftiness of Satan. But we must regularly consult him. In everything. His word is a "lamp unto [our] feet" (Ps. 119:105 KJV), not a spotlight into the future. He gives enough light to take the next step.

Glory Days are such because we learn to hear God's voice telling us to turn this way or that way. "Your own ears will hear him. Right behind you a voice will say, 'This is the way you should go,' whether to the right or to the left" (Isa. 30:21 NLT).

Refer every decision to the tribunal of heaven. Like David you can ask God to "bend low and hear my whispered plea" (Ps. 31:2 TLB). Wait until God speaks before you act. Be patient. Monitor your impulse. "I will instruct you and teach you in the way you should go; I will guide you with My eye" (Ps. 32:8). If you feel a check in your heart, heed it and ask God again. This is the only way to outwit the devil's deceit.

Consult God in everything, and . . .

Call on God for great things. Joshua did. The alliance with the Gibeonites quickly proved to be troublesome. The other kings of Canaan saw them as traitors and set out to attack them. Five armies bore down on the people of Gibeon. They were outnumbered. But since they had an alliance with Joshua, they asked the Hebrews to help. Because he had given his word, Joshua had no choice but to come to their rescue.

> So Joshua ascended from Gilgal, he and all the people of war with him, and all the mighty men of valor. And the Lord said to Joshua, "Do not fear them, for I have delivered them into your hand; not a man of them shall stand before you." Joshua therefore came upon them suddenly, having marched all night from Gilgal. (Josh. 10:7–9)

The five kings never stood a chance. Apparently they did not expect Joshua to respond with such fervor. They turned and ran with Hebrews hot on their heels. As Joshua's army thundered behind them, the clouds began to thunder above them. "Large hailstones" fell from the sky in a divine carpet bombing (v. 11).

Joshua saw the hailstones falling and anticipated the sun setting. It was midday. *We need more time,* he realized. Nightfall would give the enemies a chance to regroup. If he had just a few more hours of daylight, he could win the battle and strike a decisive blow. So he began to pray. He had failed to pray about the Gibeonites. He didn't make the same mistake twice.

> The day God gave the Amorites up to Israel, Joshua spoke to God, with all Israel listening:
>> "Stop, Sun, over Gibeon;
>> Halt, Moon, over Aijalon Valley."
>> And Sun stopped,

Moon stood stock still

Until he defeated his enemies.

(You can find this written in the Book of Jashar.) The sun stopped in its tracks in mid sky; just sat there all day. There's never been a day like that before or since—GOD took orders from a human voice! Truly, GOD fought for Israel.

Then Joshua returned, all Israel with him, to the camp at Gilgal.
(vv. 12–15 MSG)

This was a stunning, unprecedented prayer. The narrator, knowing his readers would be shocked at the story, referred to the Book of Jashar, an extrabiblical volume that contained stories of the Hebrew people. He was stating, in effect, "If you find this hard to believe, check it out in the Book of Jashar."

The verse that deserves your highlighter is 14. "GOD took orders from a human voice!" God, in his providence, pressed the solar Pause button. He chose to hear and heed Joshua's request. Might he do something similar for us?

My friend Greg Pruett believes that God will. He is trained as an engineer, linguist, and Bible translator. But his most significant contribution might be in the area of "extreme prayer." In his book by that name, he relates how he returned from Guinea, West Africa, to assume the role as president of Pioneer Bible Translators. It was 2008. The great recession was sucking dollars out of the economy and confidence out of the public. The ministry's financial chart indicated a free fall toward insolvency. Greg had no experience in leading such an organization. He had no tangible place to cut expenses. Resources were few, and the donors were disappearing.

Greg knew of only one response: prayer. "That's when I began to learn not to pray about my strategies, but to make prayer *the* strategy."[4]

In July he wrote a half-page letter to his teammates worldwide, calling them to prayer. He urged them to stand before God's throne with specific and bold requests. They did. Greg described the result:

> When I saw the end-of-the-year report, I knew God had heard our prayers. My eyes welled up with tears . . . If a financial expert were to analyze this graph, he or she would put their finger on the month of July and say, "What did you do right here? Whatever it was, you need to do a lot more of that." I searched in vain for a tangible explanation. I wanted to find trends to explain how it worked, so we could do it again. I never could . . . I just know [God] provided. All I had was God and prayer.[5]

Maybe God and prayer are all you have too. Like Joshua, you face battles. Five kings are bearing down upon you. Discouragement, deception, defeat, destruction, death. They roar into your world like a Hells Angels motorcycle gang. Their goal is to chase you back into the wilderness.

Don't give an inch. Respond in prayer—honest, continual, and audacious prayer.

You are a member of God's family. You come to God not as a stranger but as an heir. Confidently approach his throne. Earnestly make your requests known to him not because of what you have achieved but because of what Christ has done. Jesus spilled his blood for you. You can spill your heart before God.

Jesus said if you have faith, you can tell a mountain to go and jump into the sea (Mark 11:23). What is your mountain? What is the challenge of your life? Call out to God for help. Will he do what you want? I cannot say, but this I can: He will do what is best.

During the season I was writing this book, I had the opportunity to lead a group of five hundred people to Israel. One morning we had a Bible study on the southern steps of the Temple Mount. This precious ascent remains much the way it was two thousand years ago when Jesus and his disciples gathered there.

Our group sat with the eastern sun on their left shoulders and the temple wall to their backs. Behind them was the Dome of the Rock, the third-holiest site in the Muslim faith.

For my lesson I chose a phrase out of John 3:16 (NIV)—"one and only." Since we were sitting where Jesus stood, it seemed only right to consider Jesus' claim that he was God's one and only Son. The fact that we sat in the shadow of a mosque dedicated to Muhammad only elevated the contrast.

A few minutes into the message a mysterious voice began to mock my words. It was high pitched and eerie. Each time I said "one and only," it mimicked "one and only." When I said the name "Jesus," the voice, heavy with an accent, scoffed, "Jesus." The interruptions had all the earmarks of a spiritual conflict. Christ being proclaimed. Christ being mocked. Jesus' authority declared. Jesus' authority belittled.

I could tell that the voice came from behind the people. I searched the walls but saw nothing. The people began to turn and look for the origin of the voice, as did the guides and guards. No one could isolate it.

The more I preached, the louder the voice parroted. For fear of conceding defeat to this odd force, I didn't stop. The second point in my message was "Christ, the one and only ruler." I seized the opportunity. Rather than teach the point, I prayed and proclaimed it: "Jesus is the supreme authority of this place, any place, and every place, which, by the way, includes any demons, servants of hell, and Satan himself. You are not welcome in this gathering!" I repeated this declaration several times until the crowd began to applaud and shout "Amen!"

The dissenting voice was suddenly silent. As if a switch had been flipped, it stopped. We completed the Bible lesson in peace. I later asked a tour guide if the culprit had been found. "We tried," he told me, "but we could not find him." The guide had no explanation.

I do.

A person might chalk up the silence of the scoffer to coincidence. I don't. I see it as Providence. When the authority of Christ is proclaimed, the work of Satan must stop. Any demonic tongue must mute itself at the presence of truth.

That includes any force that is seeking to drive you out of the Promised Land.

Call on God. Declare the name of Jesus.

"Ask and it will be given to you" (Matt. 7:7 NIV).

"If you believe, you will get anything you ask for in prayer" (Matt. 21:22 NCV).

Yes, it is a battle, but you do not fight in vain.

Consult God in all things. Call on him for great things. And bring extra sunscreen, because the day of victory will last long into the night.

13

YOU BE YOU

Joshua 11–22

No one else has your "you-ness." No one else in all history has your unique history. No one else in God's great design has your divine design. No one else shares your blend of personality, ability, and ancestry. When God made you, the angels stood in awe and declared, "We've never seen one like that before." And they never will again.

You are heaven's first and final attempt at you. You are matchless, unprecedented, and unequaled.

Consequently, you can do something no one else can do in a fashion no one else can.

Others can manage a team but not with your style. Others can cook a meal but not with your flair. Others can teach kids, tell stories, aviate airplanes. You aren't the only person with your skill. But you are the only one with your version of your skill. You entered the world uniquely equipped. You were "knit . . . togethe r . . . woven together in the dark of the womb" (Ps. 139:13, 15 NLT), "intricately *and* curiously wrought [as if embroidered with various colors]" (v. 15 AMP).

Call it what you wish. A talent. A skill set. A gift. An anointing.

A divine spark. An unction. A call. The terms are different, but the truth is the same: "The Spirit has given each of us a special way of serving others" (1 Cor. 12:7 CEV).

Each of us—not some of us, a few of us, or the elite among us. Each of us has a *special way*—a facility, a natural strength, a tendency, or an inclination. A beauty that longs to be revealed and released. An oak within the acorn, pressing against the walls of its shell. This "special way" is quick to feel the wind at its back. It is the work for which you are ideally suited.

This is your destiny. This is you at your best. When you stand at the intersection of your skill and God's call, you are standing at the corner of Promised Land Avenue and Glory Days Boulevard. This is Canaan.

Many people stop short of their destiny. They settle for someone else's story. "Grandpa was a butcher, Dad was a butcher, so I guess I'll be a butcher." "Everyone I know is in farming, so I guess I'm supposed to farm." Consequently, they risk leading dull, joyless, and fruitless lives. They never sing the song God wrote for their voices. They never cross a finish line with heavenward-stretched arms and declare, "I was made to do this!"

They fit in, settle in, and blend in. But they never find their call. Don't make the same mistake.

"It is God himself who has made us what we are and given us new lives from Christ Jesus; and long ages ago he planned that we should spend these lives in helping others" (Eph. 2:10 TLB). Your existence is not accidental. Your skills are not incidental. God "shaped each person in turn" (Ps. 33:15 MSG).

Uniqueness is a big message in the Bible. And—this may surprise you—it is a huge message of the book of Joshua. In fact, one could argue that the majority of its chapters advance one command: know your territory and possess it.

Joshua's first goal was to establish Israel in Canaan by taking the land, neutralizing the enemy armies, and eliminating the major seats of authority. The lists of conquered kings in chapter 12 proclaim: the land is taken. The rest of the book urges: now take the land. Each tribe was given a distinct territory and/or assignment.

The inheritance was for everyone. All the Hebrews were welcomed to Canaan—the old, the young, the feeble, the forceful. The inheritance was universal.

But the assignments were individual. They are listed in detail in Joshua 13–21. If you can't fall asleep tonight, read these chapters. The book moves from an action novel to a land survey. The pages make for dull reading unless, of course, you stand to inherit something.

Since all the Israelites stood to receive an inheritance, they all stood alert as Joshua assigned the territory. Each tribe was called forward. Reuben, Gad, Manasseh . . . Each territory was different. Judah's parcel was large and central. Dan's section was smaller and coastal. Even the assignments were unique. The tribe of Levi was given not land but God himself as their inheritance. Their role was to lead worship and teach the Torah.

The big message was this: No one gets everything. But everyone gets something. Drive out the remaining enemies. Build your farms. Cultivate your fields. Find your lot in life and indwell it.

Joshua wasn't the only commander to distribute territory. Jesus distributes gifts that are unique as well. The apostle Paul explained it this way: "[God] has given each one of us a special gift through the generosity of Christ. That is why the Scriptures say, 'When he ascended to the heights, he led a crowd of captives and gave gifts to his people'" (Eph. 4:7–8 NLT). The apostle was using the metaphor of a victorious king. It was common in Paul's day for the conquering monarch to return to his palace with prisoners and treasures in tow. He celebrated his conquest by giving gifts to his people.

So did Jesus. Having defeated sin and death on the cross, he ascended to heaven, took his rightful place at the right hand of God, and "gave gifts to his people."

What a delightful thought! Jesus, eternally crowned, distributing abilities and skills. "The kingdoms of this world have become the kingdoms of our Lord and of His Christ, and He shall reign forever and ever" (Rev. 11:15).

Joshua said,

"Tribe of Judah, take the high country."
"Manasseh, occupy the valleys."
"People of Gad, inhabit the land east of the Jordan."

Jesus says,

"Joe, take your place in the domain of medicine."
"Mary, your territory is accounting."
"Susan, I give you the gift of compassion. Now occupy your territory."

Everybody gets a gift. And these gifts come in different doses and combinations. "Each person is given something to do that shows who God is" (1 Cor. 12:7 MSG).

Our inheritance is grace based and equal. But our assignments are tailor-made. No two snowflakes are the same. No two fingerprints are the same. Why would two skill sets be the same? No wonder Paul said, "Make sure you understand what the Master wants" (Eph. 5:17 MSG).

Do you understand what your Master wants? Do you know what makes you, you? Have you identified the features that distinguish you from every other human who has inhaled oxygen?

You have an "acreage" to develop, a lot in life. So "make a careful exploration of who you are and the work you have been given, and then sink yourself into that" (Gal. 6:4 MSG).

You be you. No one else is like you. Imagine a classroom of kids on a given day in a given school. Ten of the twenty-five students are fighting to stay awake. Ten others are alert but ready to leave. Five students are not only awake and alert, but they don't want the class to end. They even do odd things like extra homework or tutoring. What class was that intriguing to you?

"If anyone ministers, let him do it as with *the ability* which God supplies" (1 Peter 4:11, emphasis mine). Ability reveals destiny. What is your ability? What do you do well? What do people ask you to do again? What task comes easily? What topic keeps your attention?

Your skill set is your road map. It leads you to your territory. Take note of your strengths. They are bread crumbs that will lead you out of the wilderness. God loves you too much to give you a job and not the skills. Identify yours.

What you do for a living should conform to your design. Few situations are more miserable than a job misfit. Yet few maladies are more common. One study stated that only 13 percent of all workers find their work truly meaningful.[1] No wonder commuters look so grumpy. Nearly nine out of ten of them don't want to go to work. Imagine the impact this unhappiness has on health, family, and performance. If a person spends forty or more hours a week plodding through a job he or she does not like or care about, what happens?

Find something you like to do, and do it so well that people pay you to do it. For twenty years I was the senior minister of our church. I was in the thick of it all: budgets, personnel issues, buildings, hiring, and firing. I was happy to fill the role. But I was happiest preaching and writing. My mind was always gravitating toward the next sermon, the next series. Even during committee meetings, *especially* during committee meetings, I was doodling on the next message.

As the church increased in number, so did the staff. More staff meant more people to manage. More people to manage meant spending more time doing what I didn't feel called to do.

I was gradually becoming one of the grumpy 87 percent.

I was blessed to have options. I was equally blessed to have a church that provided flexibility. I transitioned from senior minister to teaching minister.

When I became teaching minister, a few people were puzzled.

"Don't you miss being the senior minister?"

Translation: Weren't you demoted?

Earlier in my life I would have thought so. But I have come to see God's definition of promotion: a promotion is not a move up the ladder; it is a move toward your call. Don't let someone "promote" you out of your call.

Look for ways to align your job with your skills. This may take time. This may take several conversations with your boss. This may take trial and error . . . but don't give up. Not every tuba player has the skills to direct the orchestra. If you can, then do. If you can't, blast away on your tuba with delight.

"Stir up the gift of God which is *in you*" (2 Tim. 1:6, emphasis mine).

You be you. Don't be your parents or grandparents. You can admire them, appreciate them, and learn from them. But you cannot be them. You aren't them. "Don't compare yourself with others. Each of you must take responsibility for doing the creative best you can with your own life" (Gal. 6:4–5 MSG).

Jesus was insistent on this. After the resurrection he appeared to some of his followers. He gave Peter a specific pastoral assignment that included great sacrifice. The apostle responded by pointing at

John and saying, "'Lord, what about him?' Jesus answered, 'If I want him to live until I come back, that is not your business. You follow me'" (John 21:21–22 NCV). In other words, don't occupy yourself with another person's assignment; stay focused on your own.

A little boy named Adam wanted to be like his friend Bobby. Adam loved the way Bobby walked and talked. Bobby, however, wanted to be like Charlie. Something about Charlie's stride and accent intrigued him. Charlie, on the other hand, was impressed with Danny. Charlie wanted to look and sound like Danny. Danny, of all things, had a hero as well: Adam. He wanted to be just like Adam.

So Adam was imitating Bobby, who was imitating Charlie, who was imitating Danny, who was imitating Adam.

Turns out, all Adam had to do was be himself.[2]

Stay in your own lane. Run your own race. Nothing good happens when you compare and compete. God does not judge you according to the talents of others. He judges you according to yours. His yardstick for measuring faithfulness is how faithful you are with your own gifts. You are not responsible for the nature of your gift. But you are responsible for how you use it.

Do not be like the Hebrews. I wish I could report that each tribe moved quickly into its land, drove out the inhabitants, and put the acreage to good use. They didn't. In some cases the tribes did not drive out the enemies:

"The children of Israel did not drive out the Geshurites or the Maachathites" (Josh. 13:13).

"They did not drive out the Canaanites who dwelt in Gezer" (16:10).

"[They] could not drive out the inhabitants . . . [T]he Canaanites were determined to dwell in that land" (17:12).

Your enemy, the devil, is determined to linger in your land as well. You must drive him out. He will lure you with thoughts of greed, power, or jealousy. Be on your guard.

Other tribes fell victim not to Canaanites but to their own laziness. Long after Joshua had distributed the land, seven of the tribes were still in the military camp. Joshua had to scold them. "How long will you neglect to go and possess the land which the LORD God of your fathers has given you?" (18:3).

How do we explain their indolence? They marched out of the wilderness and conquered the land. Yet when the time came to inherit their unique parcels, they grew lazy.

Don't make the same mistake. You are an heir with Christ of God's estate. He has placed his Spirit in your heart as a down payment. What God said to Joshua, he says to you: "Every place that the sole of your foot will tread upon I have given you" (1:3).

But you must possess it. You must deliberately receive what God so graciously gives.

All that you need to enter your Promised Land is to walk by faith. So walk! Move forward! Find your lot in life and live in it.

You be you.

14

THE GOD-DRENCHED MIND

Joshua 14:6–15

You'll never have a problem-free life. Ever. You'll never drift off to sleep on the wings of this thought: *My, today came and went with no problems in the world*. This headline will never appear in the paper: "We have only good news to report."

You might be elected as president of Russia. You might discover a way to e-mail pizza and become a billionaire. You might be called out of the stands to pinch-hit when your team is down to its final out of the World Series, hit a home run, and have your face appear on the cover of *Sports Illustrated*.

Pigs might fly.

A kangaroo might swim.

Men might surrender the remote control.

Women might quit buying purses.

It's not likely. But it's possible.

But a problem-free, no-hassle, blue-sky existence of smooth sailing? Don't hold your breath.

Problems happen. They happen to rich people, sexy people, educated people, sophisticated people. They happen to retired people, single people, spiritual people, and secular people.

All people have problems.

But not all people see problems the same way. Some people are overcome by problems. Others overcome problems. Some people are left bitter. Others are left better. Some people face their challenges with fear. Others with faith.

Caleb did.

His story stands out because his faith did. Forty-five years earlier when Moses sent the twelve spies into Canaan, Caleb was among them. He and Joshua believed the land could be taken. But since the other ten spies disagreed, the children of Israel ended up in the wilderness. God, however, took note of Caleb's courage. The man's convictions were so striking that God paid him a compliment that would make a saint blush. "My servant Caleb has a different spirit and follows me wholeheartedly" (Num. 14:24 NIV). How would you like to have those words on your résumé? What type of spirit catches the eye of God? What qualifies as a "different spirit"?

Answers begin to emerge during the distribution of the lands west of the Jordan.

"Then the children of Judah came to Joshua in Gilgal" (Josh. 14:6). Every Hebrew tribe was represented. All the priests, soldiers, and people gathered near the tabernacle. Eleazar, the priest, had two urns, one containing the tribal names, the other with lists of land parcels.[1] Yet before the people received their inheritance, a promise needed to be fulfilled.

> And Caleb the son of Jephunneh the Kenizzite said to him: "You know the word which the LORD said to Moses the man of God concerning you and me in Kadesh Barnea." (v. 6)

I'm seeing a sturdy man with sinewy muscle. Caleb, gray headed and great hearted, steps forward. He has a spring in his step, a sparkle in his eye, and a promise to collect. "Joshua, remember what Moses told you and me at Kadesh Barnea?"

Kadesh Barnea. The name stirred a forty-five-year-old memory in Joshua. It was from this camp that Moses sent out twelve spies, and it was in this camp that Moses heard two distinct reports.

All twelve men agreed on the value of the land. It flowed with milk and honey. All twelve agreed on the description of the people and the cities. Large and fortified. But only Joshua and Caleb believed the land could be overtaken.

Read carefully the words that Caleb spoke to Joshua at the end of the military campaign. See if you can spot what was different about Caleb's spirit. (Here's a hint: italics.)

Caleb . . . said to [Joshua]: "You know the word which *the* Lord said to Moses the man of God concerning you and me in Kadesh Barnea. I was forty years old when Moses the servant of *the* Lord sent me from Kadesh Barnea to spy out the land, and I brought back word to him as it was in my heart. Nevertheless my brethren who went up with me made the heart of the people melt, but I wholly followed *the* Lord my God. So Moses swore on that day, saying, 'Surely the land where your foot has trodden shall be your inheritance and your children's forever, because you have wholly followed *the* Lord my God.' And now, behold, *the* Lord has kept me alive, as He said, these forty-five years, ever since *the* Lord spoke this word to Moses while Israel wandered in the wilderness; and now, here I am this day, eighty-five years old. As yet I am as strong this day as on the day that Moses sent me; just as my strength was then, so now is my strength for war, both for going out and for coming in. Now therefore, give me this mountain of which *the* Lord spoke in that day; for you heard in that day how the Anakim were there, and that the cities were great and fortified. It may be that *the* Lord will be with me, and I shall be able to drive them out as *the* LORD said." (vv. 6–12, emphasis mine)

What name appears and reappears in Caleb's words? The Lord. The Lord. The Lord. The Lord. The Lord. The Lord. The Lord. The Lord. The Lord. Nine references to the Lord! Who was on Caleb's mind? Who was in Caleb's heart? What caused him to have a different spirit? He centered his mind on the Lord.

What about you? What emphasis would a transcript of your thoughts reveal? The Lord? Or the problem, the problem, the problem, the problem? The economy, the economy? The jerk, the jerk?

Promised Land people do not deny the presence of problems. Canaan is fraught with giants and Jerichos. It does no good to pretend it is not. Servants like Caleb aren't naive, but they immerse their minds in God-thoughts.

Imagine two cooking bowls. One contains fresh, clean water. The second contains battery acid. Take an apple and cut it in half. Place one half of the apple in the bowl of clean water. Place the other half in the bowl of battery acid. Leave each in its respective bowl for five minutes, and then pull out the two halves. Which one will you want to eat?

Your mind is the apple. God is good water. Problems are battery acid. If you marinate your mind in your problems, they will eventually corrode and corrupt your thoughts. But thoughts of God will preserve and refresh your attitudes. Caleb was different because he soaked his mind in God.

The psalmist showed us how to do this. He asked, "Why are you cast down, O my soul? And why are you disquieted within me?" (Ps. 42:5). He was sad and discouraged. The struggles of life threatened to pull him under and take another victim. But at just the right time, the writer made this decision: "Hope in God, for I shall yet praise Him . . . I will remember You from the land of the Jordan, and from the heights of Hermon, from the Hill Mizar" (vv. 5–6).

There is resolve in those words. "I shall yet . . . I will remember You." The writer made a deliberate decision to treat his downcast soul with thoughts of God. *Everywhere I go, I will remember you—from Jordan to Hermon to Mizar.*

In your case the verse would read, "From the ICU to the cemetery, to the unemployment line, to the courtroom, I will remember you."

There is nothing easy about this. Troubles pounce on us like rain in a thunderstorm. Finding God amid the billows will demand every bit of discipline you can muster. But the result is worth the strain. Besides, do you really want to meditate on your misery? Will reciting your problems turn you into a better person? No. But changing your mind-set will.

"Stop allowing yourselves to be agitated and disturbed" (John 14:27 AMP). Instead, *immerse your mind in God-thoughts.*

When troubles come our way, we can be stressed and upset, or we can trust God. Caleb could have cursed God. He didn't deserve the wilderness. He had to put his dreams on hold for four decades. Still, he didn't complain or grow sour. When the time came for him to inherit his property, he stepped forward with a God-drenched mind to receive it.

"Set your minds and keep them set on what is above (the higher things)" (Col. 3:2 AMP). When giants are in the land, when doubts swarm your mind, turn your thoughts to God. Your best thoughts are God-thoughts.

He is above all this mess!

He is "the Most High over all the earth" (Ps. 83:18 ESV).

Moses announced, "Who among the gods is like you, LORD? Who is like you—majestic in holiness?" (Ex. 15:11 NIV).

The psalmist asked, "Who in the skies is comparable to the LORD? Who among the sons of the mighty is like the LORD?" (Ps. 89:6 NASB).

Isaiah wrote, "Holy, holy, holy is the LORD of hosts; the whole earth is full of His glory!" (Isa. 6:3). God is not just holy or holy, holy; he is holy, holy, holy. Wholly unlike us.

Pain does not plague him.

The economy does not faze him.

The weather does not disturb him.

Elections do not define him.

Diseases do not infect him.

Death cannot claim him.

He has resources we do not have, wisdom we've never imagined. And he is "able to do exceedingly abundantly above all that we ask or think" (Eph. 3:20).

Stare at the mountain less and at the Mountain Mover more. Ponder the holiness of God. Let his splendor stun you and inspire you. And . . .

Turn a deaf ear to doubters. Ignore the naysayers. Cover your ears when the pessimists crow. People have a right to say what they want. And you have a right to ignore them. Just because someone sings the blues, you don't have to join the chorus.

Caleb and Joshua were outnumbered ten to two, but they still believed in God's power. "My brethren who went up with me made the heart of the people melt, but I wholly followed the LORD my God" (Josh. 14:8). Caleb chose to ignore the ten doubters and believe anyway.

Let's take our cue from Caleb. Disregard the lethal disbelief of cynics.

This is no sanction for rudeness or isolation. When people express their sincere struggles or questions, help them. But some folks do not want to be helped. They prefer the wilderness. They traffic in misery, manufacture unhappiness, and spurn growth. They would rather pull you down than let you pull them up. Don't let them. Don't loiter with vultures. They eat death and vomit it on anyone who will listen. Don't let them puke on you.

Caleb didn't. He filled his mind with faith and took on a God-size challenge.

When Moses sent Caleb to spy out the land, Caleb saw something that troubled him. The town of Hebron. Hebron held a special spot in the history of the Hebrews. It was the only piece of land that Abraham ever owned. Abraham buried his wife there. He was buried there. So were Isaac, Rebekah, and Jacob.

Hebron was a sacred site.

But on the day Caleb first saw it, the holy hill was inhabited by unholy people. This occupation bothered Caleb. To see the burial place of Abraham disrespected and disregarded? It was more than he could take.

So Caleb asked Moses for Hebron.

Caleb did not ask for Jerusalem, perched on Mount Moriah. Caleb did not ask for the Valley of Eshcol, where grapes grew as large as plums. He spoke not of Jericho or Jordan. He wanted Hebron. Hebron, beneath whose oaks Abraham had slept. Whose soil had known the visitation of angels. Whose earth entombed the holiest family.

Caleb, the man with a different spirit, had a secret desire. "Just give Hebron to me; I'll take care of it." Moses took the request to God. God gave the answer, and Caleb was given the land. And forty-five years later, at the age of eighty-five, the old soldier was ready to inhabit Hebron. "Give me this mountain of which the LORD spoke in that day" (14:12).

Last sighting of Caleb had him turning his face toward Hebron, where he did what he promised to do. He chased the enemy and reclaimed the city.

Caleb wanted to do something great for God. He lived with a higher call.

How high is yours? Maybe the reason your problems feel so great is because your cause is too small. Perhaps you need to *set your mind on a holy cause*.

I have a friend who makes regular medical mission trips to a remote jungle clinic in order to treat the disadvantaged. He is a retired surgeon with an ample income. He could spend every day of his life in ease and luxury. But he focuses on supporting the health clinic for his own good. "I need a cause that is greater than cable TV and Cadillacs," he said. "If I focus on my comfort, nothing can satisfy me. But when I focus on the concerns of God, I am a happy man." My friend functions out of a God-drenched mind.

If your problems are great, then your cause is too small. When your cause is great, the problems begin to shrink.

Do you have a holy cause? A faith worth preserving? A mission worth living for? Ask God to give you a Hebron to claim to his glory. An orphanage to serve. A neighbor to encourage. A needy family to feed. A class to teach. Some senior citizens to encourage. It really is better to give than receive. In the kingdom of Christ we gain by giving, not taking. We grow by helping, not hurting. We advance by serving, not demanding. Want to see your troubles evaporate? Help others with theirs.

You'll always face problems. But you don't have to face them in the same way. Instead:

Immerse your mind in God-thoughts.

Turn a deaf ear to doubters.

Set your mind on a holy cause.

Once you find your mountain, no giant will stop you, no age will disqualify you, no problems will defeat you. After all, you and Caleb have something in common. You have a different spirit.

You are a Promised Land person.

15

NO FALLING
WORDS

Joshua 21:43–45

I was comfortably seated in the exit row of the plane when a passenger coming down the aisle called my name. He was a tall, light-haired fellow who appeared to be about fifty years old and on a business trip. He introduced himself. Because of the chaos of boarding a flight, we couldn't chat. But this much I gathered. He had heard me speak some years earlier, had appreciated my books, and would love to talk someday.

I returned the greeting and settled in for the trip. About an hour later I felt a tap on my shoulder. I turned. It was the fellow who had greeted me in the aisle. He'd scribbled a message on a napkin and handed it to me.

Max,

Six summers ago Lynne and I buried our twenty-four-year-old daughter. This came about following a lake accident and two weeks on life support. We didn't see this coming. How do you go on a summer vacation with four and come back home with three?

Friends, some of whom had buried precious children, rallied around our family. A country lawyer with his encouraging message that "God means you good, not harm" was one of those encouraging voices. Several of your books were given to Lynne and me . . .

We prayed for a miracle. I wanted her made new, her smile and brilliance restored. To unplug our daughter from life support was very, very hard. Although the decision was painful, we were confident that we were doing the right thing in laying her in the arms of a mighty God. He knew our pain.

His best work may not have been restoring Erin to this life but his assistance for Lynne and me to let him have her. He made our daughter better than new. He restored my Erin to his eternal presence. That is his best work!

This was not a lightweight hope. This was an assurance: "Let me have your Erin. I've got her now."

God's children reflecting the very nature of God became his presence around us. Our faith is getting us through this.

Faith is a choice.[1]

I read the napkin testimony several times. I wanted to know, how does this happen? How does a dad bury a daughter and believe, so deeply believe, that God meant him good not harm, that God had received his daughter in his loving arms, that God did his best work in the hearts of sorrow? The napkin could have easily borne a different message. One of anger and bitterness. One of disappointment and despair. One full of hurt, even hate, toward God. What made this message different?

Simple. This grieving dad believes God's promises. "Faith is a choice," he concluded.

It is.

And Promised Land people risk the choice. When forced to stand at the crossroads of belief and unbelief, they choose belief. They place one determined step after the other on the pathway of faith. Seldom with a skip, usually with a limp. They make a conscious decision to step toward God, to lean into hope, to heed the call of heaven. They press into the promises of God.

Joshua's story urges us to do likewise. In fact, one might argue that the central message of the book is this headline: "God keeps his promises. Trust him."

> So the LORD gave to Israel all the land of which He had sworn to give to their fathers, and they took possession of it and dwelt in it. The LORD gave them rest all around, according to all that He had sworn to their fathers. And not a man of all their enemies stood against them; the LORD delivered all their enemies into their hand. Not a word failed of any good thing which the LORD had spoken to the house of Israel. All came to pass. (Josh. 21:43–45)

These three verses are the theological heart of the book of Joshua. They rise up like trumpets at the end of the narrative. "Don't miss this! Attention everyone. God keeps his word!" The writer pounds the point in triplicate. Three times in three verses he declares: *God did what he said he would do.*

1. "The LORD gave . . . all . . . He had sworn to give" (v. 43).
2. "The LORD gave . . . rest . . . according to all that He had sworn to their fathers" (v. 44).
3. "Not a word failed of any good thing which the LORD had spoken . . . All came to pass" (v. 45).

One commentator was so taken by that last statement that he entitled his Joshua study *No Falling Words.*[2]

We live in a world of falling words. Broken promises. Empty vows. Pledges made only to be retracted. Assurances given, then ignored. They were spoken with great fanfare. "I'll always love you." "Count on us to recognize good work." "Till death do us part."

But words tend to tumble. They are autumn leaves in November's wind. You've heard your share.

But you'll never hear them from God. In a world of falling words, his remain. In a life of broken promises, he keeps his. "The Lord's promise is sure. He speaks no careless word; all he says is purest truth, like silver seven times refined" (Ps. 12:6 TLB).

God is a covenant-keeping God.

Want proof? The narrator tells us to look to history. "The LORD gave to Israel all the land of which He had sworn to give to their fathers" (Josh. 21:43). Specifically, God gave Abraham a promise. "Then the LORD appeared to Abram and said, 'To your descendants I will give this land'" (Gen. 12:7).

That was six hundred years earlier! Who believed it would happen? When Abraham died, the only land he owned was Sarah's cemetery plot. His descendants were sharecroppers at best, slaves at worst, in Egypt for four centuries. Moses led them near but never into Canaan.

How many grizzled-bearded sons of Abraham looked to the stars and prayed, *God, will you keep your promise?*

The answer from the pages of Joshua is yes.

God promised to bless Abraham and through Abraham's seed all the nations of the earth. "I will bless you and make your name great; and you shall be a blessing. I will bless those who bless you, and I will curse him who curses you; and in you all the families of the earth shall be blessed" (Gen. 12:2–3). This was the promise partially fulfilled in Joshua. And this is the promise completely fulfilled in Jesus. In him all the nations are blessed. In Jesus every person has hope and the possibility of redemption. No wonder the apostle Paul wrote, "All the promises of God find their Yes in [Jesus]" (2 Cor. 1:20 ESV).

Our God is a promise-keeping God. Others may make a promise and forget it. But if God makes a promise, he keeps it. "He who promised is faithful" (Heb. 10:23 NIV).

Does this matter? Does God's integrity make a difference? Does his faithfulness come into play? When your daughter is on life support, it does. When you're pacing the ER floor, it does.

When you are wondering what to do with every parent's worst nightmare, you have to choose. Faith or fear, God's purpose or random history, a God who knows and cares or a God who isn't there? We all choose.

Promised Land people choose to trust God's promises. They choose to believe that God is up to something good even though all we see looks bad. They echo the verse of the hymn:

> *His oath, His covenant, His blood,*
> *Support me in the whelming flood.*[3]

Nothing deserves your attention more than God's covenants. No words written on paper will ever sustain you like the promises of God. Do you know them?

To the bereaved: "Weeping may stay for the night, but rejoicing comes in the morning" (Ps. 30:5 NIV).

To the besieged: "The righteous person may have many troubles, but the LORD delivers him from them all" (Ps. 34:19 NIV).

To the sick: "The LORD sustains them on their sickbed and restores them from their bed of illness" (Ps. 41:3 NIV).

To the lonely: "When you pass through the waters, I will be with you" (Isa. 43:2 NIV).

To the dying: "In my Father's house are many rooms . . . I go to prepare a place for you" (John 14:2 ESV).

To the sinner: "My grace is sufficient for you" (2 Cor. 12:9 NIV).

These promises are for your good. "And because of his glory and excellence, he has given us great and precious promises. These are the promises that enable you to share his divine nature and escape the world's corruption caused by human desires" (2 Peter 1:4 NLT).

Press into God's promises. When fears surface, respond with this thought: *But God said* . . . When doubts arise, *But God said* . . . When guilt overwhelms you, *But God said* . . .

Declare these words: "You have rescued me, O God who keeps his promises" (Ps. 31:5 TLB). Turn again and again to God's spoken covenants. Search the Scriptures like a miner digging for gold. Once you find a nugget, grasp it. Trust it. Take it to the bank. Do what I did with the promise of the pilot.

Not long after I met the note-giving gentleman on the plane, I took another flight. On this occasion a note did not come my way, but bad weather did. The flight into Houston was delayed by storms. We landed at the exact time the final flight into San Antonio was scheduled to depart. As we taxied toward the gate, I was checking my watch, thinking about hotels, preparing to call and tell Denalyn of my delay, grumbling at the bad break.

Then over the loud speaker a promise. "This is the pilot. I know many of you have connections. Relax. You'll make them. We are holding your planes. We have a place for you."

Well, I thought, *he wouldn't say that if he didn't mean it.* So I decided to trust his promise.

I didn't call Denalyn.

I stopped thinking about hotels.

I quit checking my watch.

I relaxed. I waited my turn to get off the plane and set my sights on my gate. I marched through the concourse with confidence. Hadn't the pilot given me a promise?

Other people in the airport weren't so fortunate. They, also victims of inclement weather, were in a panic. Travelers were scrambling, white faced and worried. Their expressions betrayed their fear.

Too bad their pilot hadn't spoken to them. Or perhaps he had and they hadn't listened.

Your Pilot has spoken to you. Will you listen? No, I mean *really* listen? Let his promises settle over you like the warmth of a summer day. When everyone and everything around you says to panic, choose the path of peace. In this world of falling words and broken promises, do yourself a favor: take hold of the promises of God.

My friend Wes did. You'll look a long time before you'll find a better man than Wes Bishop. He had a quick smile, warm handshake, and serious weakness for ice cream. For more than thirty-five years he kept the same job, loved the same wife, served the same church, and lived in the same house. He was a pillar in the small Texas town of Sweetwater. He raised three great sons, one of whom married my daughter Jenna. Wes never even missed a day of work until a few months ago when he was diagnosed with brain cancer.

We asked God to remove it. For a time it appeared that he had. But then the symptoms returned with a vengeance. In a matter of a few weeks, Wes was immobilized, at home, in hospice care.

The sons took turns keeping vigil so their mom could rest. They placed a baby monitor next to Wes's bed. Though he'd hardly spoken a word in days, they wanted to hear him if he called out.

One night he did. But he didn't call for help; he called for Christ. About one o'clock in the morning, the youngest son heard the strong voice of his father in the monitor. "Jesus, I want to thank you for my life. You have been good to me. And I want you to know, when you are ready to take me, I am ready to go." As it turned out, those were the final words Wes spoke. Within a couple of days Jesus took him home.

I want that kind of faith. Don't you? The faith that turns to God in the darkest hour, praises God with the weakest body. The kind of faith that trusts in God's promises. The kind of faith that presses an ink pen into an airline napkin and declares, "Faith is a choice. And I choose faith."

16

GOD FIGHTS
FOR YOU

Joshua 23

Nadin Khoury was thirteen years old, five foot two, and weighed, soaking wet, probably a hundred pounds.

His attackers were teenagers, larger than Nadin, and out-numbered him seven to one.

For thirty minutes they hit, kicked, and beat him.

He never stood a chance.

Khoury's mom had recently moved the family to Philadelphia from Minnesota. She had lost her job as a hotel maid and was looking for work. In 2000 she'd escaped war-torn Liberia. Nadin Khoury, then, was the new kid in a rough neighborhood with a mom who was an unemployed immigrant—everything a wolf pack of bullies needed to justify an attack.

The hazing began weeks earlier. They picked on him. They called his mother names. They routinely pushed, shoved, and ambushed him. Then came the all-out assault on a January day. They dragged him through the snow, stuffed him into a tree, and suspended him on a seven-foot wrought-iron fence.

Khoury survived the attack and would have likely faced a few more except for the folly of one of the bullies. He filmed the pile-on and posted it on YouTube. A passerby saw the violence and chased away the bullies. Police saw it and got involved. The troublemakers landed in jail, and the story reached the papers.

A staffer at the nationwide morning show *The View* read the account and invited Khoury to appear on the broadcast. He did. As the video of the assault played on the screen behind him, he tried to appear brave, but his lower lip quivered. "Next time maybe it could be somebody smaller than me," he said.

Unbeknownst to him, the producer had invited some other Philadelphians to appear on the show as well. As the YouTube video ended, the curtain opened, and three huge men walked out, members of the Philadelphia Eagles football team.

Khoury, a rabid fan, turned and smiled. One was All-Pro receiver DeSean Jackson. Jackson took a seat on the couch as close to the boy as possible and promised him, "Anytime you need us, I got two linemen right here." Khoury's eyes widened saucer-like as Jackson signed a football jersey and handed it to him. Then, in full view of every bully in America, he gave the boy his cell phone number.[1]

From that day forward Khoury has been only a call away from his personal bodyguards. Thugs think twice before they harass the kid who has an NFL football player's number on speed dial.

Pretty good offer. Who wouldn't want that type of protection?

Joshua did. Brutal and bloodthirsty enemies occupied the Promised Land. Joshua's men were untested. His leadership was unproven. Yet in spite of the odds, God guaranteed the conquest. "No man shall be able to stand before you all the days of your life; as I was with Moses, so I will be with you. I will not leave you nor forsake you" (Josh. 1:5).

It was as if God told him, "Jericho has its thick, tall walls? True, but you have me. The Amorites have home-field advantage? They do, but you have the King of heaven on your side. The enemies have more chariots, experience, and artillery? Yes, they are strong, but I am stronger still. And I will not leave you or forsake you."

God gives you the same promise. In fact, the writer of Hebrews quoted the words in his epistle: "For [God] has said, 'I will never leave you or forsake you.' So we can say with confidence, 'The Lord is my helper; I will not be afraid. What can anyone do to me?'" (13:5–6 NRSV).

That last question is a troubling one. *What can anyone do to me?* You know the answers. "Lie to me." "Deceive me." "Injure me." "Terrorize me." "Bully me."

But the Scripture asks a different question. If the Lord is your helper, what can anyone do to you?

The Greek word for "helper" in this passage is *boētheia*, from *boē*, which means "a shout," and *theō*, which means "to run."[2] When you need help, God runs with a shout, "I'm coming!" He never leaves you. Ever! He never takes a break, takes a nap, or takes time off for vacation. He never leaves your side.

The job market is flat? True. But God is your helper. Your blood cell count is down? Difficult for sure, but the One who made you is with you. The world is rife with conflict? Indeed it is. Still, the Almighty will never leave you or forsake you.

Consequently, everything changes! Since God is strong, you will be strong. Since he is able, you will be able. Since he has no limits, you have no limits. With the apostle you can boldly say, "The LORD is my helper; I will not fear. What can man do to me?" (v. 6).

But there is more. The biggest—and best—news of Joshua is this: God not only stays with you . . . he fights for you.

Not only does God desire that you live the Promised Land life, but he fights for you so you can. This was the main point of Joshua's victory speech. Envision the commander as he stands before his army to deliver one of his final messages.

"I am old," he begins, "advanced in age . . . [T]his day I am going the way of all the earth" (Josh. 23:2, 14). He was 110 years old when he died (24:29), so he must have been nearly that age as he spoke.

He has a rush of white hair and a chest-length beard. His back is stooped, but his voice is strong. He stands on a rock and looks out over a valley full of faces. When he lifts his hand to speak, their voices fall silent. He led them out of the wilderness, through the Jordan River, into Canaan. When Joshua speaks, they listen.

Joshua has seen every significant moment of the last half century. "You have seen all that the LORD your God has done," he announces to his soldiers (23:3).

Oh, the stories they could tell. The Jordan River opened, and the Jericho walls fell. The sun stood still, and the enemies scattered. The Hebrews inhabited farms they did not plow. They ate from vineyards they did not plant. And Joshua in his final words wants to make sure they have gotten the message: "The LORD your God is He who has fought for you" (v. 3).

The Hebrews took the land not because of their skill but God's. Throughout the book of Joshua, God does the fighting.

In his call to battle Joshua told his men, "Go in to possess the land which the LORD your God is giving you to possess" (1:11).

Then again: "The LORD your God is giving you rest and is giving you this land" (1:13).

On the eve of the Jordan crossing, Joshua declared, "The LORD will do wonders among you" (3:5).

As they stood on the western side of the river, Joshua deduced, "The LORD your God dried up the waters of the Jordan" (4:23).

On the outskirts of Jericho "Joshua said to the people: 'Shout, for the LORD has given you the city!'" (6:16).

The entire narrative reads like this: God claiming, God giving, God defending. Joshua summarized the victory by saying, "For the

LORD has driven out from before you great and strong nations; but as for you, no one has been able to stand against you to this day. One man of you shall chase a thousand, for the LORD your God is He who fights for you, as He promised you" (23:9–10).

Don't you love that image? *One man of you shall chase a thousand.* I envision a single Hebrew soldier with drawn sword racing after an entire battalion of enemies. He is outnumbered a thousand to one, but since God fights for him, they scatter like scared pigeons.

I picture the same for you. The Amorites of your life—fears, dread, hatred, and hurt—come at you like a legion of hoodlums. Yet rather than run away, you turn and face them. You unsheathe the promise of God's Word and defy the enemies of God's cause. You are a grizzly and they are rats. "Get out of here, shame! Begone, guilt! Fear of death, regrets of the past, take your puny attacks elsewhere."

This is Glory Days living. You were not made to quake in fear. You were not made to be beholden to your past. You were not made to limp through life as a wimp. You are a living, breathing expression of God. What's more, he fights for you.

Is this a new thought? You've heard about the God who made you, watches you, directs you, knows you . . . but the God who fights for you? Who blazes the trail ahead of you? Who defends you? Who collapses walls, stills the sun, and rains hail on the devil and all his forces?

Did you know that God is fighting for you? That "with us is the LORD our God, to help us and to fight our battles" (2 Chron. 32:8)? That "our God will fight for us" (Neh. 4:20)? That the Lord will "fight against those who fight against [you]" (Ps. 35:1)?

God fights for you. Let those four words sink in for a moment.

God. The CEO, President, King, Supreme Ruler, Absolute Monarch, Czar, Emperor, and Raja of all history. He runs interference and provides cover. He is impeccably perfect, tirelessly strong, unquestionably capable. He is endlessly joyful, wise, and willing. And he . . .

Fights. He deploys angels and commands weather. He stands down Goliaths and vacates cemeteries. He fights . . .

For. For your health, family, faith, and restoration. Are the odds against you? Is the coach against you? Is the government against you? Difficult for sure. But God fights for . . .

You. Yes, you! You with the sordid past. You with the receding hairline. You with the absentee dad. You with the bad back, credit, or job. He fights not just for the rich, pretty, or religious. He fights for the yous of the world. Are you a *you*?

The big news of the Bible is not that you fight for God but that God fights for you. And to know this—to know that your Father fights for you—is an unparalleled source of empowerment.

I experienced something similar many years ago after I preached my first sermon. I was fresh out of college and ready to change the world as a preacher. When I graduated, the leaders of my hometown church asked me to come and bring a sermon to the congregation.

No sermon is perfect. But a preacher's first sermon? I make no effort to defend mine. Though I gave it a good effort, I am sure I meandered and wandered. In an effort to say everything, I said very little. I don't pretend that the sermon was noteworthy.

But still, I didn't deserve the criticism from the pastor. He invited me into his study for a post-service postmortem. He'd already summoned a group of men to witness the confrontation. He pounced on the sermon like a hawk on a rat. He said that I told too many stories and used too few scriptures. I was too clever, cute, and easy on sinners. By the end of the harangue, I felt like a scolded puppy.

I tucked my tail between my legs and slouched out to the church parking lot, where my dad was waiting for me in his car. He could tell something was wrong. As I recounted the meeting, his face grew red.

His grip on the steering wheel tightened, and his lips pursed into a single line. He dropped me off at the house and said, "I'll be back soon. I need to make a visit."

It wasn't until the next day that I learned the rest of the story. My dad had pulled into the pastor's driveway. The pastor, who was watering the lawn, lowered his hose and greeted my father. Dad didn't return the nicety. He was in the preacher's face giving him what for and "how much" and demanding an explanation for the meeting.

The preacher hemmed, hawed, and eventually apologized. He called me the next day and asked my forgiveness.

Again, I am not defending the sermon. But it was a wonderful thing when my father defended me.

What's that? You wish you could say the same? You'd love for someone to rush to your defense? To stand up on your behalf? To rally against those who have railed against you?

Oh, dear child of heaven, God has!

When God became flesh, he fought for your soul. When Jesus faced the devil in the wilderness, he fought for your peace. When he stood up for the neglected, was he not standing up for you? When he died on the cross for your sins, he fought for your salvation. When he left the Holy Spirit to guide, strengthen, and comfort you, he was fighting for your life.

Miss this truth and you might as well plant a mailbox in the wilderness. You will be there a long time. But believe this, and watch the clouds begin to clear.

Believe this:

[God] won't let you stumble,
    your Guardian God won't fall asleep.
Not on your life! Israel's
    Guardian will never doze or sleep.

GOD's your Guardian,
> right at your side to protect you—
Shielding you from sunstroke,
> sheltering you from moonstroke.

GOD guards you from every evil,
> he guards your very life.
He guards you when you leave and when you return,
> he guards you now, he guards you always. (Ps. 121:3–8 MSG)

Toward the end of the invasion, the narrator of Joshua's story itemizes all the kings that the people of Israel defeated. He does so in an interesting way.

the king of Jericho	one
the king of Ai . . .	one
the king of Jerusalem	one
the king of Hebron	one (Josh. 12:9–10 NIV)

The list goes on for thirty-one lines. Each line has a name and the word *one*. It's as if the victors were placing a check mark on their list of their enemies and announcing the score.

Joshua—31

The Canaanites—0

Imagine your list. Envision the day you stand before Jesus, your Joshua, and look back over your life. "God will give to each one whatever praise is due" (1 Cor. 4:5 NLT). Your Commander will declare the final outcome of your life:

"With God's help John Doe took on the enemies of his Promised Land and drove them out.

"Greed, one!

"Explosive temper, one!

"Envy, one!

"Abused as a child yet stable as an adult.

"Tempted with drugs yet sober and steady.

"Strayed off course yet returned with vigor.

"One! One! One!"

One by one the conquests will be read and celebrated.

Every witness will rejoice at the work God did. This is God's goal for you. This is your inheritance: more victory than defeat, more joy than sadness, more hope than despair.

These days are Glory Days.

SWORDS, WARS, AND GOD

The book of Joshua is a bloody book. It does no good to pretend it isn't. Not only is something violent taking place (the killing of hordes of people), but that violence is happening to women, children, the elderly, and even animals. For many readers this violence is a barrier to embracing the book of Joshua, even the message of God.

Some attempt to get God out of this straitjacket by claiming that he didn't actually command these things but instead they were misinterpretations of God's instructions or misrepresentations by biblical writers. It is nearly impossible to go this route and retain any sense of the inspiration of Scripture, however. God's words are too clear.

So what are we to think?

Here are some thoughts that have helped me.

God knew the Canaanite people. He knew their evil. He knew their unbridled violence, and most of all, he knew it six hundred years before Joshua entered the land. Genesis 15:16 supports this claim: "In the fourth generation your descendants will come back here, for the sin of the Amorites has not yet reached its full measure" (NIV). God gave the people six centuries to respond and change their ways.

The fact that Rahab did is proof that they could have also. The fact that God accepted Rahab is evidence that he would have accepted them too.

But they did not turn. Apparently, they grew more evil over time. "They do all kinds of detestable things the LORD hates. They even burn their sons and daughters in the fire as sacrifices to their gods" (Deut. 12:31 NIV). One scholar called the Canaan of thirteenth century BC "a snake pit of child sacrifice and sacred prostitution, . . . [people who were] ruthlessly devoted to using the most innocent and vulnerable members of the community (babies and virgins) to manipulate God or gods for gain."[1]

God not only knew what they had done; he knew what they would do. His omnipotent eye saw the destruction they would wreak in the future. So he punished them. Isn't it his right to do so? Don't we, at times, want him to do so? We struggle when God doesn't punish injustice. (Why did God not intercede to stop the Holocaust?) Then we struggle when he acts justly, as he did here with the residents of Canaan.

We must approach this question with reverence: God is God. As difficult as it may be for us to embrace, he does not have to fit within our system of response. We may not understand his scheme of protection.

I'm thinking of my friend whose teenage daughter questioned her father's protection. She had a toxic boyfriend. He darkened her thought life and caused her to question all the values my friend had taught her. The boy had cast a spell over her. So my friend demanded that the two break up. When they refused, he decided to move the family. He resigned from his job and put his house on the market.

Can you imagine the tantrum his daughter threw? In her mind this was an overreaction. In his it was necessary protection.

Those who accuse God of an overreaction in Canaan might

take time to remember: We were not there. We did not know the Canaanites. We are not omniscient or sovereign, but God is.

And God is full of grace. What he commanded the Israelites to do to the Canaanites is unique in the Bible. At no other time and in no other location is Israel instructed to conduct aggressive military action. The vast majority of the stories in the Bible describe a God who rescues, redeems, and displays patience and love. Hasn't he earned our trust?

I know my answer.

It's up to you to determine yours.

By the way, God will do this again. On the Day of Judgment he will once and for all time judge all that is evil. The devil, his underlings, and all his followers will taste the final and just judgment of God. On that day, at that moment, no one will question his right to do so.

NOTES

CHAPTER 1: GLORY DAYS

1. "Conquest Confusion at Yale," Bryant G. Wood, BibleArcheology
   .org, November 20, 2012, www.biblearchaeology.org/post/2012/11/20/
   Conquest-Confusion-at-Yale.aspx#Article. Also see, Ronald B. Allen,
   "The Land of Israel," in *Israel: The Land and the People: An Evangelical Affirmation
   of God's Promises*, ed. H. Wayne House (Grand Rapids: Kregel Publications,
   1998), 17–18, 24. Caleb says he was forty years old when he went to spy
   out Canaan (Josh. 14:7). The Hebrews were in the wilderness for forty
   years (Ex. 16:35). They wandered in the wilderness for thirty-eight years
   after the spies returned, which means Caleb was seventy-eight years old
   at the beginning of the conquest. Caleb says he is eighty-five years old
   in Joshua 14:10, forty-five years of grace from God since Kadesh Barnea
   (38+7).

2. Kenneth O. Gangel, *Holman Old Testament Commentary: Joshua*, ed. Max
   Anders (Nashville: B&H, 2002), 2.

3. "To Canaan's Land I'm on My Way," *Praise for the Lord* (Nashville: Praise
   Press, 1992), 694.

4. REVEAL Spiritual Life Survey database 2007–2014. For more
   information on the REVEAL Survey see Greg L. Hawkins and Cally
   Parkinson, *Move: What 1,000 Churches Reveal About Spiritual Growth* (Grand
   Rapids: Zondervan, 2011).

5. "The Global Religious Landscape," Pew Research Religion & Public
   Life Project, December 18, 2012, www.pewforum.org/2012/12/18/
   global-religious-landscape-exec/.

CHAPTER 2: INHERIT YOUR INHERITANCE

1. Numbers 26:2, 51.

2. Eugene H. Peterson, "Introduction to Joshua," in *The Message Remix: The Bible in Contemporary Language* (Colorado Springs, CO: NavPress, 2003), 364.

3. "Amorites," JewishEncyclopedia.com, www.jewishencyclopedia.com/articles/1422-amorites.

4. In many ways Ephesians is the New Testament counterpart to the book of Joshua.

5. Dwight Edwards, *Revolution Within: A Fresh Look at Supernatural Living* (Colorado Springs, CO: WaterBrook Press, 2001), 5.

6. Spiros Zodhiates, ed., *Hebrew-Greek Key Word Study Bible: Key Insights into God's Word, New American Standard Bible*, rev. ed. (Chattanooga, TN: AMG Publishers, 2008), #4789, p.2280.

CHAPTER 3: TAKE HEED TO THE VOICE YOU HEED

1. Greg L. Hawkins and Cally Parkinson, *Move: What 1,000 Churches Reveal about Spiritual Growth* (Grand Rapids: Zondervan, 2011), 19.

2. "Global Scripture Access," United Bible Societies, www.unitedbiblesocieties.org/what-we-do/translation/global-scripture-access/.

3. "353 Prophecies Fulfilled in Jesus Christ," According to the Scriptures.org, www.accordingtothescriptures.org/prophecy/353prophecies.html.

4. Dale Ralph Davis, *Joshua: No Falling Words* (Fearn, Scotland: Christian Focus Publications, 2000), 19.

CHAPTER 4: IT'S OKAY IF YOU'RE NOT OKAY

1. "Price of Success: Will the Recycled Orchestra Last?" CBSNews.com, November 17, 2013, www.cbsnews.com/news/price-of-success-will-the-recycled-orchestra-last/Đ.

2. Joshua 2:1; 6:17, 25; Hebrews 11:31; James 2:25.

CHAPTER 5: UNPACK YOUR BAGS

1. From a conversation with Jimmy Wayne and used by permission. For a full account see Jimmy Wayne with Ken Abraham, *Walk to Beautiful: The Power of Love and a Homeless Kid Who Found the Way* (Nashville: W Publishing, 2014).

2. F. B. Meyer, *Joshua: And the Land of Promise* (London: Morgan and Scott, 1870), 35.

CHAPTER 7: CALL ON YOUR COMMANDER

1. As recounted in an interview with Joy Veron on October 10, 2013, and used by permission.

2. *Fall of Jericho: Unearthing One of the Bible's Greatest Mysteries* (Worcester, PA: Gateway Films/Vision Video, 2008), DVD.

3. H. I. Hester, *The Heart of Hebrew History: A Study of the Old Testament* (Liberty, MO: Quality Press, 1962), 143–44.

4. Adam Hamilton, "Compassion, Vision and Perseverance: Lessons from Moses," The United Methodist Reporter, January 22, 2013, http://unitedmethodistreporter.com/2013/01/22/adam-hamiltons-sermon-at-todays-national-prayer-service/. See also, Martin Luther King Jr., *Stride Toward Freedom: The Montgomery Story* (Boston: Beacon Press, 1958), xxi, 125.

5. From a conversation with Tammy Trent and used by permission.

CHAPTER 8: WALK CIRCLES AROUND JERICHO

1. "Worship of these gods [Baalism] carried with it some of the most demoralizing practices then in existence. Among them were child sacrifice, a practice long since discarded in Egypt and Babylonia, sacred prostitution, and snake-worship on a scale unknown among other peoples." G. Ernest Wright and Floyd V. Filson, *The Westminster Historical Atlas to the Bible* (Philadelphia: Westminster, 1945), 36.

2. Spiros Zodhiates, ed., *Hebrew-Greek Key Word Study Bible: Key Insights into God's Word, New American Standard Bible*, rev. ed. (Chattanooga, TN: AMG Publishers, 2008), #3423, p. 1896.

3. George V. Wigram and Ralph D. Winter, *The Word Study Concordance* (Wheaton, IL: Tyndale, 1972), 477.

4. According to the REVEAL Spiritual Life Survey database 2007–2014, this number is 89 percent. For more information on the REVEAL Survey see Greg L. Hawkins and Cally Parkinson, *Move: What 1,000 Churches Reveal About Spiritual Growth* (Grand Rapids: Zondervan, 2011).

5. Used by permission.

CHAPTER 10: NO FAILURE IS FATAL

1. Leigh Montville, "Wide and to the Right: The Kick That Will Forever Haunt Scott Norwood," SI.com, last modified September 21, 2011,

http://sportsillustrated.cnn.com/2011/writers/painful_moments_in_sports/09/09/Scott.Norwood.Super.Bowl/.

2. "The size of this group is indicated by the text as 30,000 men, which appears to be an unusually large contingent for such a secret maneuver as ambush close to the city. One plausible answer to the problem is that the text should read 'thirty officers.' This suggestion is made by R. E. D. Clark, who points out that the Hebrew word *elep,* translated 'thousand,' can also be translated as 'chief' or 'officer,' as it is translated in other passages (cf. 1 Chron. 12:23–27; 2 Chron. 13:3, 17; 17:14–19). If this were the case, then the thirty-man group was a highly selected commando unit, assigned to enter the vacated city and burn it. This view may better explain also the description of the contingent as chosen for being 'mighty men of valor'—more meaningful to a thirty-man group than to a 30,000-man unit. It should be noted here, however, that the second ambuscade definitely involved 5,000 men (8:12)." Irving L. Jensen, *Joshua: Rest-Land Won* (Chicago: Moody Press, 1966), 72.

CHAPTER 11: VOICES, CHOICES, AND CONSEQUENCES

1. David M. Howard Jr., *Joshua,* vol. 5, *The New American Commentary* (Nashville: Broadman & Holman, 2002), 212.
2. F. B. Meyer, *Joshua: And the Land of Promise* (London: Morgan and Scott, 1870), 96.
3. See also Deuteronomy 27.
4. C. S. Lewis, *Yours, Jack: Spiritual Direction from C. S. Lewis* (New York: HarperCollins, 2008), 152.
5. D. James Kennedy and Jerry Newcombe, *What If the Bible Had Never Been Written?* (Nashville: Thomas Nelson, 1998), 30–31.

CHAPTER 12: PRAY AUDACIOUS PRAYERS

1. Donald G. Bloesch, *The Struggle of Prayer* (Colorado Springs, CO: Helmers and Howard, 1988), 79.
2. Ibid., 80.
3. E. M. Bounds, *The Complete Works of E. M. Bounds on Prayer* (Grand Rapids: Baker Book House, 1990), 311–12.
4. Greg Pruett, *Extreme Prayer: The Impossible Prayers God Promises to Answer* (Carol Stream, IL: Tyndale House, 2014), 5.

5. Ibid, 69.

CHAPTER 13: YOU BE YOU

1. Art Miller, *The Power of Uniqueness* (Grand Rapids: Zondervan, 1999), 93.

2. Adapted from Joel Osteen, *Every Day a Friday: How to Be Happier 7 Days a Week* (New York: FaithWords, 2011), 131–32.

CHAPTER 14: THE GOD-DRENCHED MIND

1. F. B. Meyer, *Joshua: And the Land of Promise* (London: Morgan and Scott, 1870), 143.

CHAPTER 15: NO FALLING WORDS

1. Used with permission.

2. Dale Ralph Davis, *Joshua: No Falling Words* (Fearn, Scotland: Christian Focus Publications, 2000).

3. Edward Mote, "This Solid Rock" in *Sacred Selections for the Church: A Collection of Sacred Selections Featuring Choice Favorites Old and New* (Kendallville, IN: Sacred Selections, 1956), no. 120.

CHAPTER 16: GOD FIGHTS FOR YOU

1. Sean Alfano, "Teens Arrested after Posting YouTube Video of Beating 13-Year-Old Boy and Hanging Him from a Tree," *New York Daily News*, February 1, 2011, www.nydailynews.com/news/national/teens-arrested-posting-youtube-video-beating-13-year-old-boy-hanging-tree-article-1.137868. See also Rick Reilly, "Eagles over Wolves in a Rout," ESPN.com, last modified February 15, 2011, http://sports.espn.go. com/espn/news/story?id=6120346.

2. W. E. Vine, *Vine's Expository Dictionary of New Testament Words: A Comprehensive Dictionary of the Original Greek Words with Their Precise Meanings for English Readers* (McLean, VA: MacDonald Publishing, n.d.), 554.

AFTERWORD

1. Eugene H. Peterson, "Introduction to Joshua," in *The Message: The Bible in Contemporary Language* (Colorado Springs, CO: NavPress, 2002), 361.

QUESTIONS FOR REFLECTION

prepared by David Drury

T his study guide is designed to help you think more deeply about *Glory Days* and apply its message to your life. You'll find three sections for each chapter to assist you in the process:

Your WILDERNESS questions come from the struggling seasons of life, born of waiting, disappointment, discouragement, or heartache. For the Hebrews it was a season of wandering for forty years in the desert. Your wilderness, a wasteland of unfulfilled hopes and dreams, may feel no less barren. However hard such wandering can be, it can also be a season of spiritual growth and learning. These questions are designed to help you learn about God and yourself during your wanderings.

Your CROSSING MOMENT questions point to a symbolic Jordan River that separates your current life from the Promised Land life that is possible for you. You can cross over to this life because you have victory in all things through God, who showed his great love for you (Rom. 8:37 NCV). These questions will help you find motivation and practical steps to move out in faith and enter God's promised life.

Your PROMISED LAND questions will inspire you to see the

potential of your Promised Land life. It can be hard to imagine what a life of victory looks like. Those who have experienced victory are sometimes so humbled by it that they don't share how it feels to win over sin and shame and sickness. But victory is not only *possible* for the faithful; it is promised by God. *You can close the gap between the person you are and the person you want to be!* It's time to fully experience the Promised Land life.

May you begin to experience your Glory Days, and may you speak the words that began this book with the confidence that God's power is at work within you:

> These days are Glory Days.
> My past is past,
> my future is bright,
> God's promises are true and
> his Word is sure.
> With God as my helper,
> I will be all he wants me to be,
> do all he wants me to do,
> and receive all he wants me to receive.
> These days are Glory Days.

I

Glory Days

Reading: Joshua 21:43–45

> *In all these things we are more than conquerors through Him who loved us.*
> ROMANS 8:37

Your Wilderness

1. Perhaps you can relate to the child Max saw in the airport with the Mickey Mouse carry-on bag who said, "I can't keep up!" What are you having trouble keeping up with lately?

2. Read Exodus 17:2–4.
   - On a "grumbling to grateful" scale of one to ten (with one being grumbling and ten being grateful), where do you fall right now?
   - What present circumstances are you grumbling about too much?
   - In what way has God provided for you in the past that you could be grateful for today?

3. The Hebrews felt like grasshoppers in comparison to their enemies (Num. 13:33). What are you facing today that makes you feel powerless?

4. "Nearly nine out of ten believers languish in the wilderness." Do you count yourself among the 89 percent of churchgoers who are not fully experiencing the Promised Land life? Explain your answer.

Your Crossing Moment

5. What challenges may come when you seek to live in victory?

6. This chapter included a paraphrased version of Joshua 21:43–45 with blanks to fill in. Take the time now to speak this promise out loud, filling in your name at each blank.

The Lord gave to _____ all the life he had sworn to give. And _____ took possession of it and dwelt in it. The Lord gave _____ rest all around and not an enemy stood. Not a word failed of any good thing which the Lord had spoken to _____. All came to pass.

YOUR PROMISED LAND

7. Several scriptures are used to paint a picture of what your Promised Land life can look like. Read through these verses— Romans 8:37; 2 Corinthians 4:16–17; 2 Corinthians 5:14–17; and Colossians 3:23–24—and answer the following two questions about each one.
   - What does this passage tell you about how God sees you?
   - How does this passage inspire you toward victory?
8. Write down one of these quotes, and place it where it will remind you today of its truth:
   - "With God's help you can close the gap between the person you are and the person you want to be."
   - "Victory becomes . . . a way of life."
   - "Isn't it time for you to change your mailing address from the wilderness to the Promised Land?"

PROMISE PRAYER

Lord Jesus, my Helper, give me the strength to live out these words: "My future is bright, God's promises are true, and his Word is sure. With God as my helper, I will be all he wants me to be, do all he wants me to do, and receive all he wants me to receive. These days are Glory Days." In your name I pray, amen.

2
___

Inherit Your Inheritance

Reading: Joshua 1:1–6

I will never leave you nor forsake you. Be strong and courageous.
Joshua 1:5–6 (NIV)

Your Wilderness

1. What pictures, images, or people come to mind when you hear the word *can't?*

2. What do you think you *can't* do that you suspect God thinks you *can* do?

3. This chapter emphasizes two reasons some people don't receive their inheritance: either they don't know about their inheritance, or they don't believe in their inheritance.

   - What did you learn in this chapter about your relationship to God? How would you describe it now?

   - How has your knowledge and understanding of the inheritance concept changed? What do you now believe, and in what have you placed your faith?

   - What parts of the inheritance do you still struggle with? Take time right now to pray, and ask God to strengthen your faith. Like the man who came to Jesus for a miracle, declare, "I do believe; help me overcome my unbelief!" (Mark 9:24 NIV).

Your Crossing Moment

4. "You do not fight *for* victory. You fight *from* victory."

- Since God is already victorious, what is your role in receiving his gift of victory?
- How might this philosophy change the way you see your life?

5. From the scriptures quoted below, choose your favorite, and then read the larger context noted for each passage. How is the victory of God evident in each passage? What truths do you discover?
   - "I can do all things through Christ, because he gives me strength" (Phil. 4:13 NCV). See Philippians 4:1–20.
   - "May the God of peace . . . equip you with all you need for doing his will" (Heb. 13:20–21 NLT). See all of Hebrews 13.
   - "God has given us everything we need for living a godly life" (2 Peter 1:3 NLT). See 2 Peter 1:1–11.
   - "God's power is very great for us who believe. That power is the same as the great strength God used to raise Christ from the dead" (Eph. 1:19–20 NCV). See Ephesians 1:15–23.

Your Promised Land

6. Second Corinthians 5:17 explains that you are a "new creation" if you are "in Christ" and that everything in life is made new.
   - What would it look like for you to be "made new" in your Promised Land life?
   - How would your Promised Land life affect your relationships?
7. Your conversion to Jesus Christ is "more than a removal of sin." It is, in fact, a "deposit of power."
   - What do you need God's power to help you face in the coming days?
   - How might his power give you victory over that challenge?

Promise Prayer

Lord Jesus, my Victory, give me a believing mind and an obedient heart today. Move my spirit from one of defeat to one of victory. Help me know that I do not fight a battle I cannot win but that instead you have already given me the victory, for you are my victory! In your powerful name I pray, amen.

3

TAKE HEED TO THE VOICE YOU HEED

Reading: Joshua 1:7–18

> *I take joy in doing your will, my God, for your*
> *instructions are written on my heart.*
> PSALM 40:8 (NLT)

YOUR WILDERNESS

1. When have you struggled to read the Bible? Why did you find it difficult?
   - Are there parts of the Bible you have trouble believing? If so, give some examples.
   - What Bible story encourages you most? Why?
2. The Bible was written not by a scribe in an office but by "kings in palaces, shepherds in tents, and prisoners in prisons." Real people facing the kind of challenges you face in life wrote the Bible.
   - What is your favorite Bible story of someone overcoming a great challenge?
   - Why is that portion of Scripture particularly meaningful in your life? How might it apply to the challenges you face today?

YOUR CROSSING MOMENT

3. "All Scripture is inspired by God and is useful for teaching, for showing people what is wrong in their lives, for correcting faults, and for teaching how to live right" (2 Tim. 3:16 NCV).

- How have you found Scripture to be useful for correcting faults? What insights or guidelines for living have you found in Scripture?
- This verse says that Scripture is *useful*. How do you *use* the Bible? Brainstorm other ways you might use Scripture to enhance your daily walk.

4. Read the list of negative characteristics found in 2 Timothy 3:1–5. Which of these could apply to you?
   - What would be the opposite characteristic of the one(s) you chose?
   - In what specific ways could you live out that positive characteristic today?

YOUR PROMISED LAND

5. It would have been easy for Joshua to become distracted by the many other voices around him, but he needed to listen to the one voice that mattered most, the voice of God.
   - What voices in your world don't speak the truth of Scripture?
   - How might you minimize the impact of those voices on your life?
   - What voices around you echo the truth of Scripture?
   - What favorite passage of Scripture inspires you the most?

6. Imagine your victorious, Promised Land life. Describe the place of the Bible in your Promised Land life.
   - How will you make the Bible a priority?
   - How will you interact with the Bible?
   - What are the effects of meditating on the Bible?
   - How will you know that God's Word has taken root in your spirit?
   - Is there any reason you cannot have that Promised Land life now?

PROMISE PRAYER

Lord Jesus, my Word, speak to me with your clear voice in the middle of so many distractions. In your Word you've given me all that is necessary for me to believe today. Help me to hear it. To hear you. Speak, Lord; your servant is listening. In your name I pray, amen.

4

It's Okay If You're Not Okay

Reading: Joshua 2

> *Our hearts melted in fear and everyone's courage failed because of you, for the LORD your God is God in heaven above and on the earth below.*
>
> RAHAB IN JOSHUA 2:11 (NIV)

Your Wilderness

1. Have you ever felt undeserving of a better life?
   - What failures or limitations have made the Promised Land life seem out of reach for you?
   - What does Romans 3:23–24 say about those who deserve this better life?
2. Rahab is honored in Hebrews 11 for her great faith; she's listed along with prophets, patriarchs, priests, judges, and kings. Note the humble origins of each of the following heroes and how God used them despite their past mistakes or challenging circumstances:
   - Jacob in Genesis 27. Describe the way Jacob secured the birthright. Have you manipulated people or circumstances for your own benefit? What was the result of your actions?
   - Moses in Exodus 2:1–10. How was Moses at risk in his first moments of life? Were there times in your early life that you were at risk?
   - Gideon in Judges 6:11–18. How does Gideon describe his

feelings of unworthiness? What is the source of your feelings of unworthiness?

- Samuel in 1 Samuel 1. Samuel's birth was miraculous, but think about how Hannah felt before she conceived. Have you ever waited a long time for an answer to prayer and finally received the answer you hoped for?
- David in 1 Samuel 16:1–13. What signs indicate that the family was overlooking David at this sacrifice? Have you been ignored or disregarded because of your status or age?

Your Crossing Moment

3. Compare the account of what the priests did with the ark in Joshua 3:14–17 with the story of Rahab hanging a scarlet cord out her window in Joshua 2:17–21.
   - What reasons might God have to ask for an act of good faith before providing deliverance?
   - Has he ever asked you for this kind of step of faith? How did you respond? How do you hope to respond in the future?
   - What steps of faith are you feeling led toward today?
   - Is there anything you use to signal your faith in God or mark yourself for him?
4. Rahab was found to be a woman of great faith despite the circumstances of her life (Josh. 2:9–11).
   - Recall a rough spot in your life when God showed up. How was that situation similar to Rahab's? How did you respond? What was the outcome?
   - How do you imagine Rahab's life changed after being saved (see Josh. 6:25)?

Your Promised Land

5. Read Matthew 1:5.
   - Why do you think God made Rahab, a former prostitute, the

great-great-grandmother of King David and therefore an ancestor of Jesus himself?

- As with Rahab's choice to act in faith by signaling with the red cord, what decisions are you making today that could be felt for generations to come?

6. The Samaritan woman in John 4 had no position of influence; she was a woman in the margins of her society. But after just one conversation with Jesus, she became a great witness to her people.

- What happened in this encounter with Jesus that changed her? What can that teach us about helping others encounter Jesus?
- If God's power and victory become more active in your life, whom could you influence?

PROMISE PRAYER

Lord Jesus, my Rescuer, remind me today that, because of your forgiveness, my past doesn't disqualify me from your promises. Show me how to intentionally and boldly step into a new Promised Land life that is designed by you. In your holy name I pray, amen.

5

UNPACK YOUR BAGS

Reading: Joshua 3

> *When you reach the banks of the Jordan River, take*
> *a few steps into the river and stop there.*
> JOSHUA 3:8 (NLT)

YOUR WILDERNESS

1. Jimmy Wayne's packed bag indicated that he hadn't fully settled in. If people were to observe you, would they see any signs that you aren't yet fully settled into the family of God?
   - Do you have doubts about yourself that keep you in a spiritual wilderness?
   - What doubts do you have about God?
   - What do you need to embrace about God's character in order to feel safe unpacking your bags?
2. The Hebrews could have crossed over to the Promised Land forty years before they did, but they missed that opportunity because they doubted God.
   - Describe a time in your life when you regretted a missed opportunity to grow spiritually.
   - What would you do differently if given a second chance?
   - What did you learn from that missed opportunity? How does that knowledge equip you to seize opportunities today?

YOUR CROSSING MOMENT

3. The priests merely "dipped in the edge of the water" (Josh. 3:15).

- When you get into a swimming pool for the first time, do you dip your feet for a while, wade in slowly, dive in from the side, or even drop in with a cannonball from the diving board?
- Which of the above swimming-pool entrances best describes the way you take steps of faith?
- Think about a time you stepped out in faith. How did that affect your faith and your relationship with God?
- What small steps of faith has God pointed you toward? Did you find these steps difficult to obey? How did God bless them?

4. God stopped the water thirty miles upriver from the Israelites' crossing, far out of their sight.
   - Describe a time that God protected you or provided for you by actions faraway in time or location.
   - How can you thank him for that provision?

Your Promised Land

5. The chapter discussed three passages that describe God's compelling protection. Look up Romans 8:38–39, Colossians 1:13, and John 10:28.
   - Do you ever worry that you might lose your position as a child of God? If so, how do these verses encourage you?
   - What would it take for you to be "convinced" (Rom. 8:38 NIV) of the truths in these verses?
6. "Like the Hebrews we have been dramatically delivered."
   - What is your deliverance story? When did God rescue you?
   - How does thinking about God's goodness in the past make you feel about the future? How does this affect your relationship with God?

Promise Prayer

Lord Jesus, my Savior, remind me that, regardless of my experiences, I remain a redeemed child of God. May your deliverance define me as I come to understand your grace more and more. My life has meaning because of the cross and your work there. Continue to refine me in your salvation. In your name I pray, amen.

6

Don't Forget to Remember

Reading: Joshua 4:1–5:12

> *He did this . . . so you might fear the LORD your God forever.*
> JOSHUA 4:24 (NLT)

YOUR WILDERNESS

1. In what ways have you felt the attacks of the Enemy? What sins have held you in bondage?
   - Has God given you victory over these already? How have you praised him for it?
   - Have you yet to experience victory over some sins? How might thinking of it as a spiritual battle change your perspective on seeking victory?
2. Take time now to think about your life story.
   - When have you experienced highs and lows based on decisions you made?
   - At what times have you experienced significant struggles because of someone else's choices?

YOUR CROSSING MOMENT

3. Joshua and Caleb waited for forty years to cross the Jordan River into the Promised Land again.
   - How long have you been waiting to experience a life of victory?
   - What's been holding you back from entering your Canaan?
4. Read Ephesians 6:12–16.

- Have you ever fought against "people on earth" (NCV)? Have you ever fought against "spiritual powers" (NCV)? How can you tell the difference?
- Is part of "the full armor of God" (v. 13 NIV) missing in your life today? The belt of truth? The breastplate of righteousness? The shoes of peace? The shield of faith?
- What would help you remember to don your full spiritual armor when you face trials?

YOUR PROMISED LAND

5. In Joshua 4, God commanded Joshua to tell a dozen men to take a stone from the Jordan riverbed. Then Joshua made an altar with those stones in order to remember what God had done.
   - Pinpoint a time in your life when you clearly saw God's faithful hand at work. How easy is it for you to forget that experience when facing a new challenge?
   - What are you doing to keep that memory in mind? If you have a journal from that time, consider rereading it. If the memory is tied to a specific location, visit that spot.
6. God also commanded the Hebrews to remember whose they were. Take a look at this list of names that God calls you. Which of these do you most identify with? Which do you need to fully embrace in the Promised Land?
   - child (John 1:12)
   - friend (John 15:15)
   - redeemed (Rom. 3:23–24)
   - coheir (Rom. 8:17; Gal. 4:7)
   - new creation (2 Cor. 5:17)
   - chosen, holy, and blameless (Eph. 1:4)
   - God's workmanship (Eph. 2:10)

PROMISE PRAYER

Lord Jesus, my Deliverer, remind me throughout this day of the grace you have given me in days gone by. Help me remember that you have a clear plan for my life. I need not worry when I remember whose I am. In your name I pray, amen.

7

Call On Your Commander

Reading: Joshua 5:13–15

What do you want your servant to do?
Joshua 5:14 (NLT)

Your Wilderness

1. Several examples of "versus" are cited in this chapter: David versus Goliath, Elijah versus Jezebel, John versus the Roman Empire. And the story of Joshua versus the city of Jericho begins in Joshua 5.
   - What is your "versus"? If you were to put your name in the first blank below, what would you put in the second blank? What challenge or enemy do you face?

   _____ versus _____

2. Do you feel like the underdog in this challenge?
   - In what ways does your challenge feel insurmountable?
   - How are you entering into "enemy territory" to fight this challenge?
   - Some scholars suggest that Joshua had gone by himself to inspect Jericho's walls. Think of a circumstance in which you felt alone in enemy territory. What was the outcome?

Your Crossing Moment

3. Dedicate the next few moments to worship. Let your room

---

become a chapel. Take off your shoes just as God commanded Joshua to do in Joshua 5:15.

- Any place God is present is holy ground. Is he present with you now? How do you know that?
- What assurance does Scripture give you? Start with Joshua 1:9 and Hebrews 13:5–6.

4. What is your typical posture when you call on God? How does that affect your attitude?
   - How would your words and reverence change if you bowed low to the ground in prayer?
   - Are there certain actions of worship that you hesitate to do in public? Why?
   - How would that change if you considered that God is right by your side?

YOUR PROMISED LAND

5. How are your challenges put into perspective when you spend time thinking about the fact that your Friend and Savior, Jesus Christ, is the commander of the army of God and is fighting your challenges for you?
   - "Thousands of angels" (Heb. 12:22 NIV) and maybe even tens of thousands of angels (Rev. 5:11) are waiting for the Commander's orders. How do you envision the army of God?
   - What would you like to ask Jesus, as your Commander, to have his army do for you? What's holding you back from asking? What do you need to do to let that go?

6. Near Jericho, Joshua encountered the Commander. How do you think that experience affected him?
   - Do you ever feel you're so strong that you don't need to worship? Why?
   - What specific actions can you take to remind yourself to worship God every day?

PROMISE PRAYER

Lord Jesus, my Commander, open my eyes to the vast armies who await your orders, and empower me to live with similar obedience and trust. Whatever walls I face today, help me see past the obstacles and focus on you and your power. In your powerful name I pray, amen.

8
———

Walk Circles Around Jericho

Reading: Joshua 6

> *Shout! For the Lord has given you the town!*
> Joshua 6:16 (nlt)

Your Wilderness

1. "We have strongholds in our lives. The apostle Paul used the term to describe a mind-set or attitude." Of the strongholds mentioned in this chapter, which ones do you most identify with?
   - guilt
   - resentment
   - self-pity
   - pride
   - rejection
   - defeat
   - performance
   - appearance
   - materialism

2. What other Jericho-like strongholds has the Enemy set up in your territory?
   - Why do you think these specific attitudes have taken hold in your life?
   - What is your first step toward conquering them?

———

YOUR CROSSING MOMENT

3. Reread Joshua 6. When has God asked you to take a step of faith toward demolishing a stronghold?
   - What step of faith has he called you to take that seemed too strange to obey?
   - How did God move through your faithfulness?
   - How can you keep God at the center of your struggle?
4. What does 2 Corinthians 10:3–4 say you already have at your disposal "for pulling down strongholds"?
   - Max identifies three spiritual weapons for fighting strongholds: worship, Scripture, and prayer. Which do you feel is the strongest in your life?
   - What can you do to grow in the other areas? Consider scheduling a time to listen to worship music, reading an extra Scripture passage every day, or setting aside additional time to pray just about the strongholds in your life.

YOUR PROMISED LAND

5. Think about the strongholds that you identified in questions 1 and 2.
   - How would your life be different if you didn't struggle with these attitudes and mind-sets?
   - Can overcoming one become a stepping-stone to face another? Where can you start on this journey?
6. Memorize one of these two scriptures today, and claim the victory in Jesus Christ over your strongholds.
   - "In all these things we are more than conquerors through him who loved us" (Rom. 8:37 NIV).
   - "I can do all things through Christ who strengthens me" (Phil. 4:13).

PROMISE PRAYER

Lord Jesus, my Confidence, please give me victory over the spiritual strongholds that block me in like enemy walls. Knock down my walls of fear, of anger, of bitterness, of prejudice. Please give me an attitude of joy in my Promised Land life! In your name I pray, amen.

9
—

DON'T TRUST STUFF

Reading: Joshua 7

> *Achan answered Joshua, "It's true. I sinned against*
> *GOD, the God of Israel. This is how I did it."*
> JOSHUA 7:20 (MSG)

YOUR WILDERNESS

1. Joshua 6:18–19 makes it clear that the Hebrews were not to take anything from Jericho for themselves, which was utterly contrary to the standard practice of the day. Instead, the Hebrews were to trust God to completely meet their needs.
   - What possessions do you rely on most in your life? What would be hardest to live without?
   - What part of your life do you have the most trouble entrusting to God? Is it work, family, or friendships? How about your money, your home, or your health?
   - Why do you hold so tightly to that part of your life?
   - What actions could you take to show God that you trust him with those things closest to your heart? Could you give away something dear to you this week as a signal that it is not more important to you than God?
2. Deuteronomy 8:4 and 29:5 show that God provided for the Hebrews in a seemingly small but significant way: their clothes and sandals didn't wear out for forty years!

- How has God provided for you in small ways that were still significant?
- What large challenge are you facing right now? Are you trusting God to handle it?

YOUR CROSSING MOMENT

3. Each day comes with the opportunity to obey God in big and small things.
   - What are some of the small choices you make every day to follow God's commands?
   - How does making those smaller choices prepare you to make bigger choices?
4. "It's not that the people of Ai were formidable. It's more that the Hebrew camp was poisoned."
   - What choices are you making that might poison you and your camp?
   - What is the best way for you to confess these things? Is there someone with whom you can safely share your doubts and struggles? Do so this week.

YOUR PROMISED LAND

5. Is there someone you admire who seems to trust God well with his or her life? Could you have a meal or coffee with this person? If a face-to-face meeting isn't possible, could you ask this person some questions over the phone or by e-mail? Consider asking questions like these:
   - How do you remind yourself that you can trust God?
   - What scriptures encourage you to trust God?
   - When have you failed to trust God? What did you learn from that experience?
6. "Glory Days happen to the degree that we trust him."
   - How can you increase the degree to which you trust God? Just

as you do exercises to increase your physical strength, what spiritual workout might increase your trust?

· How are you "investing in the currency of heaven"? What does that look like in your life?

PROMISE PRAYER

Lord Jesus, my King, convict me when I hold back anything from you. If any treasured thing is buried deeper in my life than you are, expose it, root it out, and make me utterly dependent on you. I trust you. In your trustworthy name I pray, amen.

10

NO FAILURE IS FATAL

Reading: Joshua 8:1–29

> *There is therefore now no condemnation to those who are in Christ Jesus, who do not walk according to the flesh, but according to the Spirit.*
> ROMANS 8:1

YOUR WILDERNESS

1. Joshua was at the end of his rope after the deep failure at Ai. He cried out to God, "Alas, Lord GOD, why have You brought this people over the Jordan at all—to deliver us into the hand of the Amorites, to destroy us?" (Josh. 7:7).
   - Why do you think God allowed Joshua to fail?
   - Have you ever responded like Joshua and wondered why God let you fail? What reasons might God have for allowing you to stumble?

2. It is one thing to fail; it is another to *feel* like a failure.
   - When have you felt the sting of failure? On a scale of one to ten, with one being a failure and ten being a success, how would you rate yourself? Why do you rate yourself that way?
   - Have your failures stuck with you? To what degree have you felt trapped in the "Leavenworth of poor self-worth"?
   - What have you learned from your failures? Can you name failures in your life that later led to success?

YOUR CROSSING MOMENT

3. "There is therefore now no condemnation to those who are

in Christ Jesus, who do not walk according to the flesh, but according to the Spirit" (Rom. 8:1).

- In what ways do you feel condemned for your failures or mistakes in life?
- If God does not condemn you, then where do those feelings of condemnation come from?
- Read Romans 8:26. How does this verse encourage you when you feel helpless?

4. In Luke 15 you can read the story of the prodigal son, who hit rock bottom. He woke up to the reality of his situation when he realized he wanted to eat the pigs' slop.

- Was there a time in your life when you had a similar realization about some situation or sin? What did it feel like to wake up?
- Have you had times of failure even after times of conviction? How did you respond? Was it easier or harder to wake up than before? James 4:6 says, "But He gives more grace." When do you need more grace from God?

Your Promised Land

5. "God's Promised Land offer does not depend on your perfection. It depends on his."

- On the left side of a sheet of paper, list the ways that you feel you have failed, that you feel unworthy, or that you see yourself as prone to mistakes.
- On the right side of the paper, note a characteristic of Jesus Christ from each of these verses: Matthew 9:36; Mark 1:41; 10:45; Luke 23:34; John 14:14; 15:12–13; and Philippians 2:8.
- How can you lean into the qualities of Jesus that you wrote on the right side of this paper?

6. How can you depend more intentionally on the perfection of Jesus?

- In what area of life do you feel you are "just getting by"? How could you more fully rely on the victory of Christ in that area?

- Choose one of the verses from question 5, and memorize it this week.

PROMISE PRAYER

Lord Jesus, my Success, remind me that you use my failures to showcase your grace. Bring me an assurance of success in your victory. Give me the strength to follow your plan of success, not my own. In your precious name I pray, amen.

11

VOICES, CHOICES, AND
CONSEQUENCES

Reading: Joshua 8:30–35

*I, the LORD your God, . . . lavish unfailing love for a thousand
generations on those who love me and obey my commands.*
EXODUS 20:5–6 (NLT)

YOUR WILDERNESS

1. "Glory Days happen when we make good choices. Trouble
   happens when we don't."
   - What is the best choice you've ever made? What is the worst?
   - What are some of the consequences of each of those good and
     bad choices?
   - What voices were you listening to when you made those
     decisions?
2. The world is filled with voices. Advice from friends. Media point-
   ing you to the next big thing. The Word of God.
   - Which voices do you listen to most often? Are you drawn to the
     loudest voices? Or the most persistent?
   - What are the consequences of heeding God's Word?

YOUR CROSSING MOMENT

3. Few self-deceptions run as deep as that of the casual Christian,

according to the book of James: "Be doers of the word, and not hearers only, deceiving yourselves" (1:22).

- Name something you know you should do out of obedience to God but are hesitating to do. Is there a command you're struggling to follow? Why do you think that is?
- Is there a lie behind the inaction that keeps you from living the Promised Land life? Are there falsehoods you believe about yourself, God, or others? How might you eliminate them today?

4. What scriptures encourage you not only to hear but to obey? Start with these passages:
   - Deuteronomy 31:6; Psalms 16:8; 46:1–3; 55:22; 86:7; Proverbs 3:5–6; Isaiah 41:10; Luke 18:27; John 14:27; 16:33; Romans 8:31; 2 Corinthians 4:17; Philippians 1:6; Colossians 3:15; 2 Timothy 1:7; and 1 Peter 5:7.
   - Pick one of these passages, write it on an index card, and place it where you will see it and read it several times a day.

YOUR PROMISED LAND

5. God promises to show "love to a thousand generations of those who love me and keep my commandments" (Ex. 20:6 NIV).
   - What effect does your obedience to God's commands have on your life? On your children's lives? On your grandchildren's lives?
   - Identify one or two commands that you have taken to heart. How do you hope your obedience will affect your community as a whole?

6. Who are the positive voices in your life, people who encourage you to pursue God?
   - How could you arrange your schedule to spend more time with these people in your weekly or monthly routines?
   - Have you expressed to any of these people how meaningful their words are? How could you do so in the coming week?

PROMISE PRAYER

Lord Jesus, my Voice, I seek your favor, but I often neglect your words. Bring me back to your Scriptures today, impress on me the meaning of the verses, and let me hear you clearly in my Promised Land life. In your name I pray, amen.

Pray Audacious Prayers

Reading: Joshua 9–10

So let us come boldly to the very throne of God and stay there to
receive his mercy and to find grace to help us in our times of need.
Hebrews 4:16 (TLB)

Your Wilderness

1. Read Joshua 9:1–18 and the treaty with the Gibeonites.
   - Have you ever felt manipulated or tricked, as Joshua was?
   - What key step did Joshua omit in making such an important decision?
   - Have you omitted this key step in a major decision in your life? Did you come to regret it?
2. What "disguises" does the Enemy use to trick you?
   - What opportunities seemed good but were, in fact, bad options in disguise?
   - In what situations are you tempted to overcommit and underdeliver?
   - Is there someone in your life who pushes or manipulates you to do things that are unwise?

Your Crossing Moment

3. Both Martin Luther and John Wesley were cited in this chapter for praying with boldness.
   - Do you know someone who prays boldly? Why do you think that person can pray so boldly?

- What are you feeling led to pray boldly about today?
4. Take time now to pray over your challenges or opportunities.
   - What can you do differently while praying today so that you increase your boldness? A change in posture? A change in tone?
   - Do you generally use certain words when you pray? Could you use different words to express your heart more deeply?

YOUR PROMISED LAND

5. What significant decisions must you make in the next month or year?
   - Consider making a personal pledge to bring these decisions to God in prayer first.
   - Do you find it difficult to bring some things to God? What holds you back? How can you find the boldness needed to bring your decisions to God?
6. "So let us come boldly to the very throne of God and stay there to receive his mercy and to find grace to help us in our times of need" (Heb. 4:16 TLB).
   - How can you "stay there" in a bold posture before God?
   - What regular routines of bold prayer can you establish this week?

PROMISE PRAYER

Lord Jesus, my Savior, I know you hear my prayers, but I sometimes don't ask enough. I doubt. I delay. Make me bold. Invite my audacious side into conversations with you so that I bring even my most daring desires and craziest dreams to you. In your name I pray, amen.

13

YOU BE YOU

Reading: Joshua 11–22

> *Don't compare yourself with others. Each of you must take responsibility*
> *for doing the creative best you can with your own life.*
> GALATIANS 6:4–5 (MSG)

YOUR WILDERNESS

1. "You are heaven's first and final attempt at you. You are matchless, unprecedented, and unequaled. Consequently, you can do something no one else can do in a fashion no one else can."
   - Describe the aspects of your personality and attributes that combine to make you "matchless."
   - Thank God for the gifts he has given you. Then consider whether you are using those gifts to their full potential. How could you further develop your gifts? How could you reinvest your gifts in the Lord's kingdom?

2. The Hebrews were lazy in certain ways and didn't fully develop their given land or drive out their enemies.
   - In what ways have you not yet developed your gifts fully?
   - What God-given abilities do you have that you could develop, apply, and use for the good of others?

YOUR CROSSING MOMENT

3. When do you feel that you're "at your best" and that you're succeeding in life?
   - What are you typically accomplishing on your best "glory days"?

- What are you typically doing on days that seem the least glorious?
4. "It is God himself who has made us what we are and given us new lives from Christ Jesus; and long ages ago he planned that we should spend these lives in helping others" (Eph. 2:10 TLB).
   - What gifts and abilities has God given you that have changed your life?
   - How are you using these gifts to help others?

YOUR PROMISED LAND

5. "No one gets everything. But everyone gets something."
   - Do you ever desire more or different gifts and abilities?
   - What abilities can you admit you don't have?
   - What is the "something" you do have that you can thank God for?
6. "Ability reveals destiny."
   - Which of your abilities might reveal something about your future?
   - How are you developing your abilities to prepare for the future?
7. "You be you."
   - How would you describe yourself?
   - Imagine how those who love and appreciate you would describe your gifts. What would they say is your strongest gift?
   - Spend some time pondering how God has placed you in situations to use the gifts he gave you.

PROMISE PRAYER

Lord Jesus, my Inspiration, give me a confidence in my skills and gifts that comes from a reliance on you. Give me true humility that comes from wisdom, where I do not think too much or too little of myself but just right—just as you made me to be. In your name I pray, amen.

Chapter 14: The God-Drenched Mind

Reading: Joshua 14:6–15

> *Now all glory to God, who is able, through his mighty power at work within us, to accomplish infinitely more than we might ask or think.*
> Ephesians 3:20 (NLT)

Your Wilderness

1. Caleb's speech in Joshua 14:6–12 repeatedly emphasizes the words "the Lord," showing that God is the main character of the story. The theme of Caleb's thoughts seems always to be "the Lord."
   - What worldly things distract you from focusing on God?
   - Is it "the economy" or "that jerk"? Is it "my mother" or "my job"? What people, circumstances, or events dominate your thoughts in a way that you would like to replace with thoughts of the Lord?
   - How might making the Lord the constant theme of your thoughts change the way you see these people, circumstances, or events that distract you?
2. For the psalmist in Psalm 42:6, "the heights of Hermon" and "the Hill Mizar" were places of intense trial and difficulty.
   - What places or situations have brought you the most trials and difficulties in life?
   - How can you consciously add God to those memories? Where can you see him working in those situations?

Your Crossing Moment

3. Colossians 3:2 (AMP) says, "Set your minds and keep them set on what is above (the higher things)."
   - What existing habits help you set your mind on things above?
   - Think of someone whose faith you admire. How might you imitate his or her God-centered focus in your life?
4. The chapter focused on three key steps in imitating Caleb's life of faithfulness to God. Let's think about each.
   - *Immerse your mind in God-thoughts.* On a scale of one to ten, with one being low and ten being high, how immersed are you in God-thoughts? What can you do today to increase that rating?
   - *Turn a deaf ear to doubters.* What habits would help you do this better?
   - *Set your mind on a holy cause.* What holy cause do you sense God calling you to set your mind on? What big thing do you want to see happen for God's glory?

Your Promised Land

5. God is "able to do exceedingly abundantly above all that we ask or think" (Eph. 3:20).
   - Think of some numbers or statistics that would represent what your Promised Land life would be like. Dream for a moment. It could be pounds lost or clients served, days sober or years in retirement. It might concern salary, investments, or a raise, but think of nonfinancial issues as well.
   - With God on your side can these things happen? What's holding you back?
   - What percentage would "exceedingly abundantly above" represent? Twenty percent more? Fifty percent more? One hundred percent more?
   - Multiply what you are asking or thinking about by that percentage, and ask God to do that—in his time and in his way.

6. "Abundantly above" in Ephesians 3:20 might mean more in quantity and also in quality.
   - Are there hints of dreams in your life that would aim higher and be more significant to others around you?
   - Can you imagine a more noble purpose for your life that God is hoping you will ask for or think about?

PROMISE PRAYER

Lord Jesus, my Holy Spirit, focus my attention on you and your ways today. Give me a different spirit, and center my mind on you. Help me view the world around me through your eyes so I might see a Promised Land beyond anything I could ask for or imagine. In your all-powerful name I pray, amen.

NO FALLING WORDS

Reading: Joshua 21:43–45

> *Not a word failed of any good thing which the*
> *LORD had spoken . . . All came to pass.*
> JOSHUA 21:45

YOUR WILDERNESS

1. In the past has someone broken his or her word to you?
    - How deeply did you trust that person before the breach?
    - How did it feel to have your trust broken?
    - Has God broken your trust at any time? What promises do you
      feel are unfulfilled in your life but could still be realized?
    - When were the promises for Israel fulfilled?
2. If you embrace the message of *Glory Days*, from time to time you will
    stand at a crossroads of belief and unbelief, and you will choose
    belief.
    - What kind of crossroads of belief and unbelief have you already
      faced? When has your faith in God been tested?
    - What crossroads do you anticipate or know are coming? What
      part of Joshua's story can prepare you for that day?

YOUR CROSSING MOMENT

3. In just a few short verses at the heart of the book of Joshua, the
    fulfilled promises of God are emphasized three times: "The
    LORD gave Israel all the land he had sworn to give" (21:43 NIV);

"The LORD gave them rest . . . according to all that He had sworn to their fathers" (v. 44); and "Not a word failed of any good thing which the LORD had spoken . . . All came to pass" (v. 45).

- Can you identify three times God kept his promises to you?
- Take time right now to pray and thank God for his love and faithfulness.

4. "Faith is a choice. And I choose faith."
   - When might you next share with your family members or friends that you have made a choice of faith and are firm in it?
   - Your friends or family may be waiting to see whether you will remain faithful in hard times. How can you prepare yourself to stand firm when that time comes?

YOUR PROMISED LAND

5. What would your life look like if it were lived with greater faith in the promises of God?
   - How might you respond in difficult times if you believed more strongly in the promises of God?
   - What troubling or addictive behaviors of yours would lose their appeal if you believed a promise from God more deeply?

6. Several promises from God were shared in this chapter. Look up a few of these in Scripture, and highlight the ones that speak to you deeply. Memorize the one that you are claiming as your promise.
   - Psalm 30:5
   - Psalm 34:19
   - Psalm 41:3
   - Isaiah 43:2
   - John 14:1–2
   - 2 Corinthians 12:9

PROMISE PRAYER

Lord Jesus, my Promise, remind me today how trustworthy you are. Convince me of your promises, and convict me with your presence. Your words do not return void and never fall to the ground. Give me an unshakable faith in them. In your holy name I pray, amen.

16

———

GOD FIGHTS FOR YOU

Reading: Joshua 23

> GOD *guards you from every evil,*
> *he guards your very life.*
> *He guards you when you leave and when you return,*
> *he guards you now, he guards you always.*
>
> PSALM 121:7–8 (MSG)

YOUR WILDERNESS

1. What has happened in your life since you began reading this book? Have you had struggles and victories? Temptations, trials, and tests?
   - In what ways is God already pulling you out of a wilderness and helping you cross over to your Promised Land life?
   - In what ways do you feel you are still on the east side of the Jordan River in your struggles?
2. In recent months how have you seen God present with you to guard your life?
   - When have you sensed that God was watching over you?
   - How has evil been unable to make you fail? Are you comfortable calling these times "victory" in Jesus Christ (who made it possible)?

YOUR CROSSING MOMENT

3. What steps of faith is God calling you to take in response to what you have learned?

———

- Brainstorm a list of a dozen or more steps of faith you could take immediately.
- Narrow the list down to the top three. Ask God to guide you in what to choose. Then start with one step.
- What can you do to stay accountable to take each of the three steps?

4. Read Psalm 121:1–8.
   - Where are you tempted to find your "help" outside of God?
   - How does verse 5 describe God's closeness to you?
   - When does God watch over you and for how long?

Your Promised Land

5. In the chapter you are described as a grizzly bear wielding God's Word, and the troubles that plague you are described as rats fleeing before you.
   - From what do you need God's protection? Now picture that challenge as a rat running away from you in God-fearing flight. How does this kind of word image help you see threats in a more appropriate way?
   - Praise the Lord for the grizzly-bear power and victory you have in him! Intentionally thank God right now for fighting for you.
6. How would you summarize what you've learned from this study on the victory Jesus Christ wins for you?

Promise Prayer

Lord Jesus, my Glory, give me an incredible sense of your victorious life today. Help me see the little ways you fight for my soul every day. Thank you for how much you do for me! I am yours, and I want your Promised Land life alive in me! In your glorious name I pray, amen.

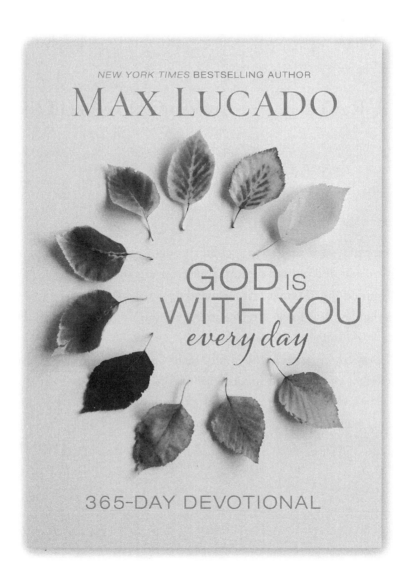

Enjoy this preview of Max's brand new daily
devotional, *God Is With You Every Day*.

Available December 2015 wherever
books and ebooks are sold.

A Prayer . . . as God's Child

For you did not receive the spirit of bondage again to fear, but you received the Spirit of adoption by whom we cry out, "Abba, Father."
ROMANS 8:15 NKJV

Father, you have made me your child through your Spirit. In your kindness you adopted me and delivered me from sin and death.

Remind me today what it means to be your child and to be free from that law. It is so easy for me to live my day on my own terms. Help me to live it in light of your grace.

I pray for my friends and family. Help them experience your love as their father and feel their inheritance in your spirit.

Thank you for accepting me as I am but not leaving me the same. In Jesus' name, amen.

Pocket Prayers

BECOME AS LITTLE CHILDREN

But Jesus said, "Let the little children come to Me, and do not
forbid them; for of such is the kingdom of heaven."

MATTHEW 19:14 NKJV

Jesus invites us to approach God the way a child approaches his or her daddy.

And how do children approach their daddies? I went to a school playground to find out.

I heard requests: "Daddy, can Tommy come home with me? I heard questions: "Are we going home?" And I heard excitement: "Daddy! Look what I did!"

Here's what I didn't hear: "Father, it is most gracious of thee to drive thy car to my place of education and provide me with domestic transportation." I didn't hear formality or impressive vocabulary. I heard kids who were happy to see their dads and eager to speak.

God invites us to approach him in the same manner. What a relief! We prayer wimps fear "mis-praying." What are the expected etiquette and dress code of prayer? What if we kneel instead of stand? What if we say the wrong words or use the wrong tone?

Jesus' answer? "Unless you are converted and become as little children, you will by no means enter the kingdom of heaven" (Matt. 18:3). Become as little children. Carefree. Joy filled. Playful. Trusting. Curious. Excited. Forget greatness; seek littleness. Trust more; strut less. Make lots of requests, and accept all the gifts. Come to God the way a child comes to Daddy.

Before Amen

Not Home Yet

"There is more than enough room in my Father's home. If this were not so, would I have told you that I am going to prepare a place for you? When everything is ready, I will come and get you, so that you will always be with me where I am."

John 14:2–3 NLT

You were born heaven-equipped with a hunger for your heavenly home. Need proof?

Consider your questions. Questions about death and time, significance and relevance. Animals don't seem to ask the questions we do. Dogs howl at the moon, but we stare at it. How did we get here? What are we here for? Are we someone's idea or something's accident? Why on earth are we on this earth?

We ask questions about pain. The words leukemia and child shouldn't appear in the same sentence. And war. Can't conflict go the way of cassette tapes and telegrams? And the grave. Why is the dash between the dates on a tombstone so small? Something tells us this isn't right, good, fair. This isn't home.

From whence come these stirrings? Who put these thoughts in our heads? Why can't we, like rabbits, be happy with carrots and copulation? Because, according to Jesus, we aren't home yet.

God's Story, Your Story

WHAT WILL HE DO WITH YOU?

"No man ever spoke like this Man!"

JOHN 7:46 NKJV

Jesus claimed to be able to forgive sins—a privilege only God can exercise (Matt. 9:4–7 NIV). He claimed to be greater than Jonah, Solomon, Jacob, and even Abraham (Matt. 12:38–42; John 4:12–14; 8:53–56 NIV). Jesus commanded people to pray in his name (John 14:13–14 NIV). He claimed his words would outlive heaven and earth (Mark 13:31 NIV) and that all authority in heaven and on earth had been given to him (Matt. 28:18–20 NIV).

Does a decent fellow say things like this? No, but a demented fool does.

Maybe Jesus was a megalomaniac. But, honestly, could a madman do what Jesus did?

Look at the devotion he inspired. People didn't just respect Jesus. They liked him; they left their homes and businesses and followed him. Men and women alike tethered their hope to his life. Impulsive people like Peter. Visionaries like Philip. Passionate men like John, careful men like Thomas, methodical men like Matthew the tax collector. When the men had left Jesus in the grave, it was the women who came to honor him—women from all walks of life, homemaking to philanthropy.

And people were better because of him. Madmen sire madmen. But Jesus transformed common dockworkers and net casters into the authors of history's greatest book and founders of its greatest movement.

What will he do with you?

God's Story, Your Story

STRUGGLES

I begged the Lord three times to take this problem away from
me. But he said to me, "My grace is enough for you. When
you are weak, my power is made perfect in you."

2 CORINTHIANS 12:8–9 NCV

We all struggle with struggles. But did you ever think that perhaps God may be using your struggles to change you? To shape you? Even to heal you?

For two years I have been asking God to remove the pain in my writing hand. Even as I write these words, I feel stiffness in my thumb, fingers, forearm, and shoulder. The doctors chalk it up to thirty-plus books written in longhand. Over the decades the repeated motion has restricted my movement, rendering the simplest of tasks—writing a sentence on a sheet of paper—difficult.

So I do my part. I stretch my fingers. A therapist massages the muscles. I avoid the golf course. I even go to yoga! But most of all I pray.

Better said, I argue. Shouldn't God heal my hand? My pen is my tool. Writing is my assignment. So far he hasn't healed me.

Or has he? These days I pray more as I write. Not eloquent prayers but honest ones. Lord, I need help . . . Father, my hand is stiff. The discomfort humbles me. I'm not Max, the author. I am Max, the guy whose hand is wearing out. I want God to heal my hand. Thus far he has used my hand to heal my heart.

So that thing you're struggling with, that you've prayed about over and over and over again . . . . could it be that God is using it to heal your heart?

Before Amen

ONLY THE BEGINNING

*Jesus said . . . "I am the resurrection and the life. The one
who believes in me will live, even though they die."*

JOHN 11:25–27 NIV

This heart will feel a final pulse. These lungs will empty a final breath. The hand that directs this pen across the page will fall limp and still. Barring the return of Christ, I will die. So will you. As the psalmist asked, "Who can live and not see death, or who can escape the power of the grave?" (Psalm 89:48 NKJV). Young and old, good and bad, rich and poor. Neither gender is spared; no class is exempt. "No one has power over the time of their death" (Ecc. 8:8 NIV).

The geniuses, the rich, the poor—no one outruns it or outsmarts it. Julius Caesar died. Elvis died. John Kennedy died. Princess Diana died. We all die. We don't escape death.

The finest surgeon might enhance your life but can't eliminate your death. The Hebrew writer was blunt: "People are destined to die once" (Heb. 9:27 NIV). Exercise all you want. Eat nothing but health food, and pop fistfuls of vitamins. Stay out of the sun, away from alcohol, and off drugs. Do your best to stay alive, and, still, you die.

Death seems like such a dead end.

Until we read Jesus' resurrection story.

"He is not here. He has risen from the dead as he said he would" (Matthew 28:6 NCV).

Death is only the beginning.

God's Story, Your Story

BELIEVE THAT HE WILL!

So all of us who have had that veil removed can see and reflect the
glory of the Lord. And the Lord—who is the Spirit—makes us more
and more like him as we are changed into his glorious image.
2 CORINTHIANS 3:18 NLT

You want your life to matter. You want to live in such a way that the world will be glad you did.

But how can you? How can I?

I have one hundred and twenty answers to that question. One hundred and twenty residents of ancient Israel. They were the charter members of the Jerusalem church (Acts 1:15 NKJV). Fishermen, some. Revenue reps, others. A former streetwalker and a converted revolutionary or two. Truth be told, they had nothing more than this: a fire in the belly to change the world.

Thanks to Luke we know how they fared. He recorded their stories in the book of Acts. Let's listen to it. That's right—listen to the book of Acts.

Hear sermons echo off the temple walls. Baptismal waters splashing, just-saved souls laughing. Hear the spoon scrape the bowl as yet another hungry mouth is fed.

Listen to the doors opening and walls collapsing. Doors into palaces, prisons, and Roman courts. And walls. The thick and spiked division between Jew and Gentile—crash! The partitions that quarantine male from female, landowner from pauper, master from slave, black African from Mediterranean Jew—God demolishes them all.

Acts announces, "God is afoot!"

Is he still? we wonder. Would God do with us what he did with his first followers?

You'd better believe that he will!

Outlive Your Life

A PRAYER . . . IN HIS IMAGE

God created mankind in his own image, in the image of God
he created them; male and female he created them.

GENESIS 1:27 NIV

O Lord, Author of my life, thank you for creating me in your image and starting my
story. Help me write it carefully and truly become like you. Come, O come, Immanuel,
and help me complete my story well. In Jesus' name, amen.

In the Manger

GRACE SEEPS IN

Create in me a clean heart, O God,
And renew a steadfast spirit within me.

PSALM 51:10 NKJV

Some years ago I underwent a heart procedure. My heartbeat had the regularity of a telegraph operator sending Morse code. Fast, fast fast. Slooooow. After several failed attempts to restore healthy rhythm with medication, my doctor decided I should have a catheter ablation. A cardiologist would insert two cables in my heart. One was a camera; the other was an ablation tool. To ablate is to burn. Yes, burn, cauterize, singe, brand. If all went well, the doctor, to use his coinage, would destroy the "misbehaving" parts of my heart.

As I was being wheeled into surgery, he asked if I had any final questions. (Not the best choice of words.) I tried to be witty.

"You intend to kill the misbehaving cells, yes?"

"That is my plan."

"As long as you are in there, could you take your little blowtorch to some of my greed, selfishness, superiority, and guilt?"

He smiled and answered, "Sorry, that's out of my pay grade."

Indeed it was, but it's not out of God's. He is in the business of changing hearts.

We would be wrong to think this change happens overnight. But we would be equally wrong to assume change never happens at all. It may come in fits and spurts. But it comes. "The grace of God that brings salvation has appeared" (Titus 2:11). The floodgates are open, and the water is out. You just never know when grace will seep in.

Grace

THE TRAGEDY OF
OLD WINESKINS

*"No one puts new wine into old wineskins; or else the new wine
bursts the wineskins, the wine is spilled, and the wineskins are
ruined. But new wine must be put into new wineskins."*

MARK 2:22 NKJV

I'll never forget Steven. I met him in St. Louis. His twenty-three years had
been hard on him, his arm scarred from the needle and his wrist scarred
from the knife. His pride was his fist, and his weakness was his girl.

Steve's initial response to love was beautiful. As we unfolded the
story of Jesus before him, his hardened face would soften and his dark
eyes would dance.

But his girlfriend would have none of it. Any changes Steve made
would be quickly muffled as she would craftily maneuver him back into
his old habits. We begged him to leave her. He was trying to put new
wine into an old wineskin.

He wrestled for days trying to decide what to do. Finally, he reached
a conclusion. He couldn't leave her.

The last time I saw Steve, he wept . . . uncontrollably. The prophecy
of Jesus was true. By putting his new wine into an old skin, it was lost.

Think for a minute. Do you have any wineskins that need to be thrown
out? Maybe yours is an old indulgence—food, clothes, sex. Or an old habit,
like gossip or profanity. Or possibly, like Steve, an old relationship. No
friendship or romance is worth your soul. Repentance means change. And
change means purging your heart of anything that can't coexist with Christ.

You can't put new life into an old lifestyle. The inevitable tragedy
occurs. The new life is lost.

On the Anvil

OUR INHERITANCE

*I pray that the eyes of your heart may be enlightened in order that you may
know the hope to which he has called you, the riches of his glorious inheritance
in his holy people, and his incomparably great power for us who believe.*
EPHESIANS 1:18–19 NIV

When you were born into Christ, you were placed in God's royal family.
"As many as received Him, to them He gave the right to become children of God" (John 1:12 NIV). Since you are a part of the family, you
have access to the family blessings. All of them. "In Him also we have
obtained an inheritance" (Eph. 1:11 NIV).

Surprised? You ain't heard nuttin' yet. In another passage the apostle
Paul described the value of your portfolio. "The Spirit Himself bears
witness with our spirit that we are children of God, and if children, then
heirs—heirs of God and joint heirs with Christ" (Rom. 8:16–17 NIV).

We are joint heirs with Christ. We share the same inheritance as
Christ! Our portion isn't a pittance. We don't inherit leftovers. We
don't wear hand-me-downs. We aren't left out in the cold with the distant cousins. In the traditions of Paul's day, the firstborn son received a
double portion while the rest of the siblings divvied up the remainder.
Not so with Christ. "Our standing in the world is identical with Christ's"
(1 John 4:17 MSG). Christ's portion is our portion! Whatever he has, we
have!

Glory Days

GOD IS STILL ON HIS THRONE

"When all that is good falls apart,
what can good people do?"
The Lord is in his holy temple;
the Lord sits on his throne in heaven.

PSALM 11:3–4 NCV

When all that is good falls apart, what can good people do? Isn't David's question ours? When illness invades, marriages fail, children suffer, and death strikes, what are we to do?

Curiously, David doesn't answer his question with an answer. He answers it with a declaration: "The Lord is in his holy temple; the Lord sits on his throne in heaven."

His point is unmistakable: God is unaltered by our storms. He is undeterred by our problems. He is unfrightened by these problems. He is in his holy temple. He is on his throne in heaven.

Buildings may fall, careers may crumble, but God does not. Wreckage and rubble have never discouraged him. God has always turned tragedy into triumph.

In our toughest times we may see what the followers of Christ saw on the cross. Innocence slaughtered. Goodness murdered. Heaven's tower of strength pierced. The apostles had to wonder, *When all that is good falls apart, what can good people do?*

God answered their question with a declaration. With the rumble of the earth and the rolling of the rock, he reminded them, "The Lord is in his holy temple; the Lord sits on his throne in heaven."

And, today, we must remember: He still is. He is still in his temple, still on his throne, still in control. What he did then, he will do still.

For the Tough Times

SATAN'S DEADLIEST TRICK

So, because you are lukewarm, and neither hot nor
cold, I will spit you out of my mouth.
REVELATION 3:16 ESV

He's a deadly snake. Satan's snake. Be on your guard.

He lurks in every dark corner and musty hole. He strikes with abandon. The old, the rich, the poor, the young—all are his prey and he seldom misses his target.

Who is this snake? Greed? Lust? Egotism? No, I'm unmasking the vilest of hell's vipers—complacence.

We're complacent to hope. Many people settle for a stale, vanilla lifestyle that peaks at age seventeen. Hope? What's to hope for? Life is a paycheck and a weekend. Nothing more.

We're complacent to death. Masked faces at a funeral endure the procession; weep at the burial; and then, a few hours later, giggle at the television comic.

We're complacent to God. Churchgoers pack the pews and sing to the back of someone's head. Fellowship is lost in formality. One, two, three times a week people pay their dues, endure a ritual, and walk out.

We're complacent to purpose. Never asking "Why am I here?" Or, worse yet, asking why and being content with no answer.

Sometimes I want to stand at the corner of the street and yell, "Doesn't anyone want to know why? Why lonely evenings? Why broken hearts? Why abandoned marriages? Why fatherless babies?" But I never yell it. I just stick my hands in my pockets and stare . . . and wonder.

The most deadly trick of Satan is not to rob us of answers. It's to steal our questions.

On the Anvil

SATURDAY

THE SIGH

Then, looking up to heaven, He sighed, and said to him, "Ephphatha," that is, "Be opened."

MARK 7:34 NKJV

As God's story becomes your story, you make this wonderful discovery: you will graduate from this life into heaven. Jesus' plan is to "gather together in one all things in Christ" (Eph. 1:10 NKJV). "All things" includes your body. Your blood-pumping heart, arm-hinging elbow, weight-supporting torso. God will reunite your body with your soul and create something unlike anything you have seen: an eternal body.

You will finally be healthy. You never have been. Even on the days you felt fine, you weren't. You were a sitting duck for disease, infections, airborne bacteria, and microbes.

I hate disease. I'm sick of it.

So is Christ. Consider his response to the suffering of a deaf mute. "He took him aside from the multitude, and put His fingers in his ears, and He spat and touched his tongue. Then, looking up to heaven, He sighed, and said to him, 'Ephphatha,' that is, 'Be opened'" (Mark 7:33–34 NKJV).

Everything about this healing stands out. The way Jesus separates the man from the crowd. The tongue and ear touching. But it's the sigh that we notice. Jesus looked up to heaven and sighed. This is a sigh of sadness, a deep breath, and a heavenly glance that resolves, "It won't be this way for long."

God's Story, Your Story

253

The Lucado Reader's Guide

Discover . . . Inside every book by Max Lucado, you'll find words of
encouragement and inspiration that will draw you into a deeper experience with
Jesus and treasures for your walk with God. What will you discover?

3:16: The Numbers of Hope
. . . the 26 words that can change
your life.
core scripture: John 3:16

And the Angels Were Silent
. . . what Jesus Christ's final days can
teach you about what matters most.
core scripture: Matthew 20–27

The Applause of Heaven
. . . the secret to a truly satisfying life.
core scripture: The Beatitudes,
Matthew 5:1–10

Before Amen
. . . the power of a simple prayer.
core scripture: Psalm 145:19

Come Thirsty
. . . how to rehydrate your heart
and sink into the wellspring of
God's love.
core scripture: John 7:37–38

Cure for the Common Life
. . . the unique things God designed
you to do with your life.
core scripture: 1 Corinthians 12:7

Facing Your Giants
. . . when God is for you,
no challenge is too great.
core scripture: 1 and 2 Samuel

Fearless
. . . how faith is the antidote to
the fear in your life.
core scripture: John 14:1, 3

A Gentle Thunder
. . . the God who will do whatever it
takes to lead his children back to him.
core scripture: Psalm 81:7

God Came Near
. . . a love so great that it left heaven
to become part of your world.
core scripture: John 1:14

Grace
. . . the incredible gift that saves
and sustains you.
core scripture: Hebrews 12:15

Great Day, Every Day
. . . how living in a purposeful way
will help you trust more, stress less.
core scripture: Psalm 118:24

The Great House of God
. . . a blueprint for peace, joy, and
love found in the Lord's Prayer.
core scripture: The Lord's Prayer,
Matthew 6:9–13

He Chose the Nails
. . . a love so deep that it chose death
on a cross—just to win your heart.
core scripture: 1 Peter 1:18–20

He Still Moves Stones
. . . the God who still does the
impossible—in your life.
core scripture: Matthew 12:20

In the Eye of the Storm
. . . peace in the storms of your life.
core scripture: John 6

In the Grip of Grace
. . . the greatest gift of all—the
grace of God.
core scripture: Romans

It's Not About Me
. . . why focusing on God will make
sense of your life.
core scripture: 2 Corinthians 3:18

Just Like Jesus
. . . a life free from guilt, fear,
and anxiety.
core scripture: Ephesians 4:23–24

A Love Worth Giving
. . . how living loved frees you
to love others.
core scripture: 1 Corinthians 13

Next Door Savior
. . . a God who walked life's
hardest trials—and still walks
with you through yours.
core scripture: Matthew 16:13–16

**No Wonder They Call Him
the Savior**
. . . hope in the unlikeliest place—
upon the cross.
core scripture: Romans 5:15

Outlive Your Life
. . . that a great God created you
to do great things.
core scripture: Acts 1

Six Hours One Friday
. . . forgiveness and healing in
the middle of loss and failure.
core scripture: John 19–20

Traveling Light
. . . the power to release the burdens
you were never meant to carry.
core scripture: Psalm 23

**When God Whispers
Your Name**
. . . the path to hope in knowing that
God knows you, never forgets you, and
cares about the details of your life.
core scripture: John 10:3

When Christ Comes
. . . why the best is yet to come.
core scripture: 1 Corinthians 15:23

You'll Get Through This
. . . hope in the midst of your hard
times and a God who uses the mess
of life for good.
core scripture: Genesis 50:20

Recommended reading if you're struggling with . . .

FEAR AND WORRY

Before Amen
Come Thirsty
Fearless
For the Tough Times
Next Door Savior
Traveling Light

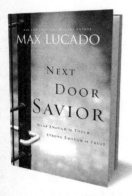

DISCOURAGEMENT

He Still Moves Stones
Next Door Savior

GRIEF/DEATH OF A LOVED ONE

Next Door Savior
Traveling Light
When Christ Comes
When God Whispers Your Name
You'll Get Through This

GUILT

In the Grip of Grace
Just Like Jesus

LONELINESS

God Came Near

SIN

Before Amen
Facing Your Giants
He Chose the Nails
Six Hours One Friday

WEARINESS

Before Amen
When God Whispers Your Name
You'll Get Through This

Recommended reading if you want to know more about . . .

THE CROSS

And the Angels Were Silent
He Chose the Nails
No Wonder They Call Him the Savior
Six Hours One Friday

GRACE

Before Amen
Grace
He Chose the Nails
In the Grip of Grace

HEAVEN

The Applause of Heaven
When Christ Comes

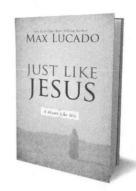

SHARING THE GOSPEL

God Came Near
Grace
No Wonder They Call Him the Savior

Recommended reading if you're looking for more . . .

COMFORT
For the Tough Times
He Chose the Nails
Next Door Savior
Traveling Light
You'll Get Through This

COMPASSION
Outlive Your Life

COURAGE
Facing Your Giants
Fearless

HOPE
3:16: The Numbers of Hope
Before Amen
Facing Your Giants
A Gentle Thunder
God Came Near
Grace

JOY
The Applause of Heaven
Cure for the Common Life
When God Whispers Your Name

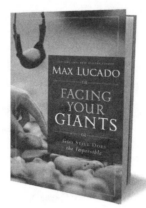

LOVE
Come Thirsty
A Love Worth Giving
No Wonder They Call Him the Savior

PEACE
And the Angels Were Silent
Before Amen
The Great House of God
In the Eye of the Storm
Traveling Light
You'll Get Through This

SATISFACTION
And the Angels Were Silent
Come Thirsty
Cure for the Common Life
Great Day Every Day

TRUST
A Gentle Thunder
It's Not About Me
Next Door Savior

Max Lucado books make great gifts!
If you're coming up to a special occasion, consider one of these.

FOR ADULTS:
For the Tough Times
Grace for the Moment
Live Loved
The Lucado Life Lessons Study Bible
Mocha with Max
DaySpring Daybrighteners® and cards

FOR TEENS/GRADUATES:
Let the Journey Begin
You Can Be Everything God Wants You to Be
You Were Made to Make a Difference

FOR KIDS:
Just in Case You Ever Wonder
The Oak Inside the Acorn
You Are Special

FOR PASTORS AND TEACHERS:
God Thinks You're Wonderful
You Changed My Life

AT CHRISTMAS:
The Crippled Lamb
The Christmas Candle
God Came Near

Tools for your Church and Small Group

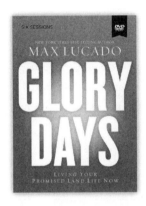

Glory Days: A DVD Study
ISBN: 978-0-7180-3603-4
$ 26.99

Max Lucado leads this six-session study of the book of Joshua and helps modern-day Christians live their Promised Land lives. This study will help small group participants leave fear and worry behind, overcome rejection, and deal with doubt through God's Word.

Glory Days Study Guide
ISBN: 978-0-7180-3597-6
$10.99

This guide is filled with Scripture study, discussion questions, and practical tools to help small-group members begin living their Promised Land lives now.

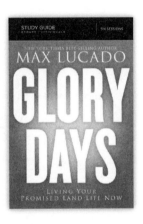

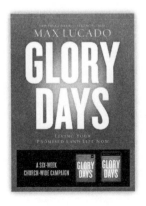

Glory Days: Church Campaign Kit
ISBN: 978-0-7180-3598-3
$59.99

The *Glory Days* Church Campaign Kit includes the six-session DVD study by Max Lucado; a study guide with discussion questions and video notes; the *Glory Days* trade book; a getting started guide; and access to all the resources a church needs to launch and sustain this six-week campaign.

Glory Days for Everyone

He Fights for You
ISBN: 978-0-7180-3790-1
$2.99

Includes forty promises featuring worship, Scripture, and guided prayers to face every stronghold in life. It's ideal for churches and ministries to use as an outreach tool.

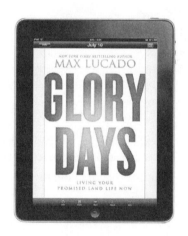

Glory Days eBook
ISBN: 978-0-7180-3790-1
$27.99

Enjoy Glory Days anywhere on your favorite tablet or electronic device.

Días de Gloria
Spanish Edition
ISBN: 978-0-7180-3412-2
$13.99

The message of Glory Days is also available for Spanish-language readers.

Make Prayer a Daily Part of Your Child's Life

9780849947483